I MISS

Hugs, Kisses, and Conversation

BY
Allen Prell

ISBN 978-1-958788-89-9 (Digital)

ISBN 978-1-958788-82-0 (Paperback)

ISBN 978-1-958788-83-7 (Hardcover)

Copyright © 2023 by Allen Prell

All Rights Reserved. No part of this publication may be reproduced, distributed, or transmitted in any form or by any means, including photocopying, recording, or other electronic or mechanical methods without the prior written permission of the publisher. For permission requests, solicit the publisher via the address below.

Publify Publishing

1412 W. Ave B

Lampasas, TX 76550

publifypublishing@gmail.com

Hugs   Kisses   Conversations

Reader, you are about to embark on an exhilarating journey. It is part memoir, part motivational and inspirational and part self-help. It is a story with two major threads: living with a spouse suffering from a chronic mental illness and its implications and second, how the author eventually made the transition from the death of his loving partner to a new and fulfilling life. This is not strictly a "how to" book. Rather, it candidly describes how one man transitioned from a dark, tragic situation to a life with a bright future. To quote him ". . .every person has a story, don't they?" His "story" includes a lot of practical, helpful advice on making those often-challenging transitions later in life.

I am making this little contribution to Allen's book not as a neophyte, but as someone who has also lived with an adult child who was mentally ill, a child who died at the tender age of 36. My wife of 55 five years and I have also had to deal with cancer five times between us. We know firsthand about suffering and the challenges that it poses. What I found in Allen's book was hope, the power of endurance and the necessity of love and compassion in all our lives. Reader, so will you!

Steve May

Dedication

Join with me for a few words as I take the podium for expressing my gratitude.

This journey is to chronicle thirty years with my wife Linda who lived with mental illness. I detail the transition to a new chapter in life with the bumps, brushes and healing along the way.

My first dedication is to my wife Jen, for encouraging me on this journey. Supportive and understanding, I can't thank her enough. Love you with all my heart.

My second acknowledgement is to my past wife Linda for whom this book was written for and about, she is at peace. It was a long journey for us.

My work your about to read was encouraged and nurtured through friends at a local cigar lounge. They are published authors, educators, the list is long and impressive. Two mentions are Fata Ariu Levi, Author of Navigators Forging a Matriarchal Culture in Polynesia, among other published work and Steve May, Author, Retired teacher and Board Member Friends of the Salem Public Library. Steve was kind enough to provide a first review of I MISS.

Finally, I thank my publisher Amanda Armstrong for her guidance during the evolution of my first book. She offered objectivity and taught me about the world of publishing.

Contents

Introduction: Meeting new people 1

Meeting my first wife, Linda 4

I MISS 32

Online Dating Sites and Social Media 55

First date, Second date 87

Meeting my current wife, Jen 91

Intimacy and Closeness 94

Keeping this PG-13 94

Moving In Together 99

The Proposal: ..... or get off the pot 104

Conclusion 111

Epilogue 120

About the Author 127

Introduction

Meeting new people

This book is not a novel or historical writing; I don't plan on developing characters or intentionally a story plot. This is a work of interest in dating later in life, filled with examples of what I found useful in some situations and examples of what I did not think through carefully in other situations. For example, I did not give much thought to how my 2 adult daughters would react to dad dating again, my mistake. But knowing that today, would it really matter or change my course of my actions or decisions? No. But as I will describe later in my work, as I was serial dating, watching two different women give my youngest daughter an introduction hug and watching the difference in body language from both her and the two women was an important lesson in body chemistry. The first woman gave her a grandma hug, a "nice to meet you" hug. The woman who is now my current wife, gave my daughter a tight, lasting, sincere "I care" hug. I remember that hug vividly to till this day; it was the same experience I had. I married the woman who gives me a sincere "I love you" bear hug lasting a minute or more several times a day. I consider myself spoiled.

My education and learning how to deal with loss

I earned my BA degree in Speech Communications (Public Speaking) and Health Science, not Journalism. I was required to write a paper in college on communications, and stupid me… chose "Why we spell the way we do"? I was, am, and will always be challenged at grammar and spelling, thank God for spell check. My thirty-page paper in college, at the time, I studied the historical meaning of English spelling today in the 21st century. I was happy, at the time, to discover that our spelling today is a mix and match of multiple cultures coming together with no real explanation or reasoning. Two, to, too…. all have a purpose and meaning in literature. Memorized at best but make no sense to me.

While reading my book, please try to understand the sensitivity of losing a loved one, finding the fun of dating again later in life, and moving forward, take the experience for what it is. Ahead is my journey of entering the dating scene after losing my wife of thirty years and jumping headfirst into the dating game again after so long. I will say, as I begin this journey, I was not expecting the recoil of my children, as I started dating three months after my wife passed. My two daughters were a bit shocked, disappointed, and even upset that I could think of dating again so soon after their mother passed away.

I had a conversation with a longtime friend (who had lost his wife ten years prior) and was in a similar situation as I found myself. I asked him why he did not date after his wife passed? He said "You are an extrovert and chatty. You make friends easily and are not intimidated by rejection". My friend's comments may very well be true, but what my children did not understand is that **I Missed:** hugs, kisses, conversation, and of course holding hands. I found attraction to a person is very individual. For men; at least for me, it is about intelligence, physical beauty, stability, and love making. Not necessarily in that order. For women, I find as I have probed this question with female friends, attraction is more about stability, personality, and genuine kindness. We don't decide who we are attracted to, our brains decide.

Meeting my first wife, Linda

It was a Saturday evening in 1985, the last weekend before I would start my first Monday, at California State University Northridge (CSUN). I was suffering from a horrible cold with laryngitis and could hardly whisper. My childhood friend and cousin, Gary, called me and asked if I would attend a "HIP HOP" dance at a local Synagogue. For those unfamiliar, a HIP HOP is, or was in those days, a dance party held at a Synagogue or Temple in the local community to help the kids stay out of trouble. This was not a group of Jewish kids who thought they would get lucky that night. The boys, like myself, were "nerds" and not the forward or promiscuous type. The girls were the typical "Jewish girl", well behaved and not at all promiscuous. I told my cousin I was not feeling great and that I wanted to pass on this "fun Jewish dance party". He said that I owed him a favor; we would attend the dance for an hour and then leave. He also mentioned, 'with you having little to no voice, perhaps a girl could get in a word or two'. Perhaps I have always had the gift of gab going back to my childhood, but it has done me well financially and led me to a career in medical sales. In my college days, I guess I was a bit chatty. I agreed and looking back at it now, glad I did attend the dance.

When we arrived at the Synagogue, the parking lot was full and we slowly and cautiously entered the building. As I predicted, there were a lot of people hugging the walls, talking, and pointing at who they thought was handsome and pretty, too shy to approach. At this time in my life, I was house sitting and doing my banking at a local B of A bank branch. Yes, I am leading to a relevant part of the story. There was a bank teller who took care of my transactions and I found her sort of cute. I never saw her away from the teller window, thus I was always seeing a shoulder to head view, but often wanted to ask her out. The day came to muster up my courage and ask her out. I went to the bank for a cash withdrawal and just before I approached her window, for the first time she walked away to the other side of the lobby and I saw a full-figured woman. A BBW, also referred to as a "Big Beautiful Woman". I decided not to ask her out. Keep this in mind for later in the book.

At the Synagogue party or Hip Hop, my cousin and I walked around the room looking at the girls and that illusive future wife. I laugh as I write that last sentence, because looking back, we were no better prepared for marriage (as we were struggling to fill our gas tanks at the time). Let's face it, I was a nerd looking for action. All of a sudden, out of the corner of my eye, I saw Tina the "bank teller" on the other side of the room. We locked eyes for a moment and she pointed at me as her two girlfriends looked over at Gary and me. Tina started walking in my direction, her friends following close behind. I admit to looking for an escape, with none immediately in sight, remembering my last encounter with her at the bank. I walked toward her to face the unknown. As we stepped within feet of each other, a big smile appeared on her face as she gave me a gentle hug and introduced my cousin and I to her girlfriends. We did the formal introductions, 'Allen is my client at the bank', as Tina introduced me to Linda and Robin. 'Allen, these are my friends, Linda and Robin.' In my mind I was thinking "hello Robin and HELLO Linda", as I was attracted to Linda's smile. I introduced Gary to the three girls: Tina, Robin, and Linda. I turned to Gary and asked him to invite Linda to dance and keep her occupied. Gary had the look of distain (he didn't want to dance). I told Gary, "I did not want to be at the dance in the first place, so please do me a favor and ask Linda to a short dance." I politely asked Tina for a dance. As I was dancing with Tina, I felt uncomfortable, keeping my eyes on Linda in the background dancing with Gary.

At the conclusion of the dance with Tina, I walked over to ask Linda for a dance. Linda asked me a couple of questions and recognized I could only speak in a whisper. She took me aside in a quiet area and told me her friend Tina liked me and wanted to ask me out. Linda asked me if I was interested in Tina. I replied, "not really". I told Linda "I only know Tina as a bank teller; but I am interested in you, Linda." At that moment Linda and I had a long conversation and she shared personal information. Two hours later, we learned we were attending the same school at California State University Northridge. She was starting her second year and I was starting my first quarter on Monday. We agreed she would meet me at the conclusion of my first class at 8:00AM. I gave her a gentle kiss and hug goodbye. Linda returned with a genuine big hug and very personal kiss. As Gary and I walked away, he teased me in a condescending tone, "...I don't want to go to a stupid dance".

On Monday morning, Linda met me outside my first class at 8:00 as planned. We walked to my second class and she asked me what I was doing that afternoon. I was planning on gathering the data for a paper at the library. She offered to help me with the library study, so I gave her my class notes at her request. When I came out of my second class two hours later, Linda was standing in the hall with a stack of books and notes attached. Again, she asked with a big smile, "What are you doing this afternoon?" I replied, "Going out with you of course." I had no idea at that time, nor could I, that this pattern would continue for two more years until my graduation. We eventually married and our relationship continued to grow and develop over the next thirty years with highs and lows from her Bi-Polar disease. If I could reverse time and go back thirty years, I still would I have married Linda, knowing now what I didn't know then.

I look back at thirty years with Linda and our two daughters and realize life has been 'more of a rollercoaster ride'. Staying on the path I did; I have the life experiences captured in so many picture books. Early on in our relationship, we were on a camping trip with my best friend Jim. Linda pulled me aside and asked to go on a short walk. We strolled down a trail in the forest with her head down, and she let out a big sigh. I remember her being very uncomfortable in what she was about to say. She looked me in the eyes and told me she had the Bi-Polar illness. I am simplifying the conversation, but even though her psychiatrist strongly urged her not to tell me about her Bi-Polar diagnosis, she felt honesty was important. My experience in the healthcare field could not have prepared me for what I didn't understand and potentially would have chosen to close my eyes to. I did not understand what mental illness was. I had no idea what it meant to live with mental illness as a patient or the stigma that goes with mental illness. Today, I look back on Linda's multiple emergency-room visits due to mania episodes and long drawn out stays in psychiatric hospitals. The eventual multiple surgeries to stabilize a very rare Cushing's Disease (a benign pituitary tumor) that afflicted Linda and later in life eventually took her life at 55 years old. I ask myself today, what I have learned in the big picture and what can I share? How can I help others experiencing the pain of mental illness?

Illness and addiction come in many different packages and each person who is afflicted presents different. I meet people in life as coworkers, friends, and neighbors and realize over time that I'm not alone in my life circumstances and struggles. My business manager from many years ago married a beautiful, smart, and engaging woman. Through a personal conversation before he got married, he mentioned his girlfriend's mother was Bi-Polar and a whack-job. I wanted to share my circumstances and decided from an employee, it was not my place. Fast forward ten years and four children later, he went through the same that I went through ten years prior. I recently asked him, "If I had a conversation with you ten years ago and shared my experiences and struggles and suggested to re-think your relationship, would you have listened?" He said, probably not and he would not have the four children he has now. His wife, as Linda was, has been hospitalized several times for mania.

A close Jewish friend met a man under her management and fell in love with a soon to be Rock Star. They worked together for several years and the romance blossomed into dating and eventually they married and had a child. After several years, he was diagnosed with Bi-Polar and as the treatments mounted, so did the medical bills. I am simplifying the romance, but in the end, she filed for divorce saying, "There is no cure for mental illness and all I can see for my future is bankruptcy and no future." Love can't concur it all.

A friend and past colleague is a smart and accomplished woman who appeared to have it all, from what I knew from her story and family life. Sitting by the pool side at a medical conference, she shared that her husband is an alcoholic. Over the next five years, I heard about her life struggles. Her husband's violent outbursts and visits to rehab to dry out. Eventually, she rented an apartment for him and filed for divorce. Several days later, the police knocked on her door and delivered the news that her husband was found in the apartment dead from drinking himself to death. Several years later, still in therapy, she blames herself for his drinking and death.

These examples are just who I am aware of. Who do you know with similar struggles? The theme of mental illness and addiction is ongoing, leaving grief in its path. How we start over and try to learn from our mistakes and break a destructive pattern is part of my book. Smart and common sense has nothing to do with your brain telling you "They are the One".

This is the beginning of my journey to heal and educate healthcare providers, Students, Pharmaceutical PSR's emergency services personnel about life with mental illness and addiction if you think it applies. Bi-Polar disease in my story to be shared, but there is a lot of cross-over with other illnesses.

Allow me to share my story and answer those questions that no book has provided me….real life.

This is a book in transition, ongoing in the sense that dating and learning each day never stops. This is my story. But every story is different. Never knowing what to expect next is the best description I can give or offer the families living with mental illness or friends who offer support. It also involves the medical system and support groups who claim to be there for a crisis when mania arises. This thought, living with mental illness could be several books in itself but I don't want to detract from the purpose of the book.

Living with my first wife and mental illness was a roller-coaster ride. I say this because the emotions the family lives with have good times along with challenges.

I remember coming home from work and Linda was upset; her last best friend and support system (since moving to Keizer fifteen years ago) had requested that Linda never reach out to her again. It turned out; her friend had witnessed Linda grabbing our youngest daughter's wrist to prevent Linda from getting her wallet to get money out of the bank. Our daughter knew her mom wasn't supposed to spend money in the state of mind she was in. Her friend gave us two different excuses, but in the end, she severed ties with Linda. This sent Linda into a deep depression. Regular medication needed to be increased and weekly therapy sessions increased. This scenario is not un-common, and explains the fragility of any mental illness, Bi-Polar disease in this case.

The manic stage of Bi- Polar disease that Linda often went into caused great stress in our life. Linda would find our family address book and start with the letter A and in alphabetical order make her way all the way through spending hours on the phone with each person. This was repeated many times during manic episodes, as I was called by those friends and relatives to have Linda committed to a hospital and seek a medication. Looking back, I can't imagine the difficulty our friends and relatives had in making that call.

When those phone calls came in that I so dreaded, I needed to make a difficult decision to take Linda to the hospital and spend hours in the hospital admission process to have Linda committed. I took this as a personal "failure" to keep her out of the hospital. Providers who work with the patients and their families have no idea the family stress of life after being released from the hospital. Linda would talk for months after being released about the patients she met and friends she made while committed. When a spouse takes a loved one into the emergency room for mania, they are immediately put into a padded room for the patient's protection and to keep the psychotic patients separated from the public. There you sit in a locked padded room for hours listening to your spouse ramble on for hours about nothing that makes any sense. Finally, a counselor enters the padded room and you are asked to leave during a psych evaluation. After an hour or two, the counselor will agree that your spouse needs to be committed or they may be polite and say admitted to the hospital. At this juncture, the counselor needs to make calls to the psych wards in the community looking for an open bed and make certain the insurance will cover the stay for an unknown period of time. Some psych wards have admission people who need to get a daily or weekly approval from the insurance to cover the hospital stay. The hospital is not a cure for mental illness, only a place to stabilize. They can call the family at any time and aske the family to pick up the loved one because of a lack of insurance coverage. Finally, after hours of waiting in the locked padded room the counselor returns with the good news that a room has been found. Now I need to take my wife to the psych ward to be committed. I have been fortunate to have a local hospital room and drive across campus and at other times un-lucky and take an hour drive to another town. When I arrived at the psych ward, I was met with multiple locked doors requiring all personal effects be locked up, cell phone, keys, and other potentially dangerous items. I waited for the admissions nurse to greet Linda and I and put us into another locked room. Thank goodness this room was not padded. The admissions nurse came into the room and explained the rules as if Linda was in the right frame of mind. I started this nightmare at 1:00PM and it was now 10:00PM. The gilt and frustration I felt can't be explained in simple words, but I will start with horrific! I went home and explained to my children that their mother in the hospital. To my surprise Linda called me later that night saying she was scared and asked when she could come home? In my experience the psych ward has two functions, to keep the patients safe and to give the family time to reflect and reset. It does not help a family reset. Two days later I got a call from Linda, when are you coming to visit and will you bring the children? The children told Linda's parents that they were going to visit their mother. My mother -in law told me "Don't you dare take my grandchildren to that crazy place". I asked my brother for his advice and it was suggested "let the kids see their mother", it can't hurt. I had a sleepless night tossing and turning trying to decide the right decision. I the end I took the children to visit Linda in the hospital. It was a smooth visit and Linda reflected she wanted to come home. "There are a lot of crazies in here. The nurse said they won't keep people committed unless they are a danger to themselves or others. Linda is neither". Upon reflection and writing this book, if I needed to make the same decision again, I would not take the children to the hospital again. Linda's hospital admissions and the children visits to the psych ward are still a topic of conversation years later. The conversation is like ripping a scab off a wound. As Linda's health progressed and deteriorated the hospital admissions became more frequent as mania became more frequent.

Each time Linda was released from the hospital, I used a home health service and paid out of pocket to have someone keep an eye on her to monitor her phone use. At the time, I asked my eldest daughter to keep the phone out of Mom's hands. My daughter remembers this event today and says she played Mommy when she was sixteen for her younger sister and mother. I regret asking my daughter to help too. It has turned into a constant reminder for us all

---

Handling the uncontrollable ups and downs

Recognizing the onset of mania & depression was observed with excessive grocery shopping and chatting with strangers. It is recognized from a professional healthcare point of view as spending with no limits to dollar value. The items purchased have no value, thus a steak can be any steak regardless of price or cut. A watch can be a ten-dollar Cascio or a ten-thousand-dollar Carita. As mentioned earlier, phone use for hours is common, often repeating the same conversation. The treatment is changing the dosage of medication over time and hospitalization if unsafe for the community. The hospitalization is difficult for a constant lack or shortage of beds and I felt obligated to visit. I remember asking myself if I should bring my daughters in to visit their mother in the hospital? My children wanted to see their mother. My in-laws suggested not to bring them to see their mother in such a fragile state. In the end, I decided to bring my children in. Today, I would not have brought them in. It was a mistake. Linda saw our youngest, didn't recognize her, and asked me why I brought in the Devil. This was a learning experience for me.

Community Stigma among friends, family, and neighbors. Advice given to me when I suggested I was thinking of moving from L.A. to a small town, it is great to live in a smaller town. Everyone is supportive of your efforts. People respect you and support you especially at a small Temple. The bad news is in a small town, everyone knows your business.

When your wife shows up at a neighbor's house, walking with a Swifter broom as a cane and asking to use the bathroom the neighbor will call the police. The small-town feel comes in when the police arrive and greets your wife, "Linda, are you sure this is your home?" This is not the time for the hospital, because she does not pose a threat to the community, only a nuisance.

Understanding medications and having a back-up plan with your doctor. This is important to be with your loved one during all therapy appointments. Not for the small talk, but at the end of the session, when it is determined the medications are working or need to be adjusted. The medications, and frequently there are several, need to be understood for what they do and what to expect from them. This is important for adjustment. If the loved one is hyper, but not manic, it is OK to give the sedative. If they are on a shopping manic episode, it is OK to give one additional pill at night. A back-up plan is to call the therapist if mania gets out of hand or sleeping sixteen hours a day. This treatment is what all hospitals work with all day long with multiple patients, but they are trained.

The long recovery and effects on the children are part of the discharge recovery and part of daily living. Bi-Polar is a long- term plan of life in general. It is not to make fun of the phrase, but it is not 'Long term planning', it is 'Life planning'. The effects on children and grandchildren as un-predictable. Each child processes their environment different. My oldest daughter to this day, says she played mommy to her sister and treats her sister as such. Therapy is a work in progress. My youngest still remembers her mother asking why did I bring the devil with me? It clearly was an age where it made an impact. My children and I never really took family vacations to National Parks, that I regret. The reason for this my brother and his wife wanted to entertain my children for the summer and took them to fancy places around the world. This was in part while Linda was in the hospital or recovering from surgery. My in-laws and brother would share summers, taking the first or second half of the season caring for the children. Years later, my brother asked if I would let him and his wife take my children for a year, to avoid the stigma of their mother, I declined. .

My in-laws took my children for weeks at a time to assist when Linda was not well. They live in Las Vegas and have many pictures at the pool. Family dynamics with my brother and in-laws were planned behind my back.

Having an emergency plan of action is important for the entire family to understand. Unfortunately, we needed to use ours. Sometimes there is not a happy ending…. A happy ever after, but a lesson learned is as rewarding.

I was at a local Cigar lounge to relax at the end of the day and share with the regulars, when my phone rang and my youngest daughter's number appeared on the screen. Immediately I felt a strange sense that something was wrong. My wife had been ill for many years and I simply let life take its course and put worries aside as a coping mechanism. The saying "all the worrying in the world won't change a thing" came to mind to keep my sanity. I answered the phone to hear my daughter's frantic voice on the line, "Mom is shaking and turning all kinds of colors. She is really sweaty."

I was not sure what was accurate or a mix of drama. I told her I would be home shortly, but I was unaware at that time how much that phone call would change the course of my life. Bittersweet is a good description as I look back on my marriage. We take for granted the hugs, kisses, conversation, and holding hands that happen naturally in a relationship. I rushed home, breaking multiple traffic laws, I'm sure, not really knowing what to expect at home. I pulled into the driveway and felt a sense of urgency. I entered the house and my daughter heard the door open, she yelled out "Dad, I don't know what happened, what do I do? What's wrong with Mom?"

I walked into our bedroom to find my wife on the floor…shaking as if having a seizure, in a pool of sweat, and shades of blue. I realized immediately, something was terribly wrong and told my daughter to call 911. I took a thermometer from the medicine cabinet and placed it under her armpit. Moments later the thermometer beeped showing 104 F. I was sure it was wrong. My daughter at that moment saw the fear in my eyes, I could not hide my concern. My daughter was witnessing a true emergency with her mother and this image would remain with her for the rest of her life.

The moments after the 911 call seemed like forever as we waited for the paramedics to arrive. I was paralyzed with fear of the unknown and didn't hear the sirens from the emergency vehicles as they arrived.

Finally, I heard a loud knock on the door. "Fire Department!" They yelled. The fire crew came into the bedroom and started the initial work-up. What was a large twenty by twenty spacious master bedroom quickly shrank when suddenly filled with the fire crew? Linda was unresponsive to questions. The lead paramedic took charge and asked me questions: How long has my wife been in this condition? What medications and dose is she taking? When was the last time she had seen her doctor? I had few answers. I don't know if you 'the reader' or anyone else you might know has been in this situation of high stress, but having questions asked from emergency personnel that require accurate answers…the chemistry in the mind changes and thinking becomes a fog.

I worked as an EMT in an ambulance when I was in college. I never really understood how people could not know the answers to simple medical questions? The emergency room doctor needed to know the details and history when I arrived at the hospital. In my case, I was on the patient's end and paralyzed with fear.

In retrospect, in the days to come, the answers to what happened that afternoon at home was simple: Linda had a pituitary failure. She had been to the doctor at ten that same morning and the doctor gave her a clean bill of health. When my daughter found Linda on the floor at 4:00PM, she had been half-way on the bed with her face buried in the mattress, but her body slipped when our daughter was trying to turn her over to keep her airway clear and not obstructed by the covers on the bed. Her body had been shut down for thirty minutes, I was now surprised she was still alive.

The paramedics took Linda to the hospital and as I arrived twenty minutes later, I found Linda sitting up in her hospital bed smiling. As I looked at the computer monitor next to her bed, I saw numbers in red all indicating dangerously high chemistry levels. Her temperature was 102 down from 104 and her potassium level was eight, "considered lethal" (Normal potassium is 4.5) and anything above 5 as very dangerous. Her Glucose was 450, well above normal. The ER doctor took me aside and told me Linda was in very, very, very critical condition. I left the hospital room to collect my thoughts of the "What if"...which was very real to me at that moment.

I came back to the intensive care unit (ICU) the next morning to visit with Linda and talk with the doctor. I gave Linda a huge hug and kiss, as I had not done in a very long time. Even as I write this, almost five year later, tears stream down my face. The hugs, kisses, conversations, and of course holding Linda's hand that I shared over the years that I took for granted would soon be gone forever. Hospital lab test results showed the glucose remained very high despite multiple doses of insulin and her potassium remained at a dangerous level of six. The doctor consulted with me, Linda, and a Nurse Practitioner who was in the room. I explained that I was in medical diagnostic lab sales and from seeing the computer screen and the red arrows all showing elevated numbers, this was not good. The doctor said he was a patient advocate, not a hospital advocate. Meaning, I do what is in the patient's best interest and not the hospital's interest. He gave Linda and I limited options. He could stop all the medications and wait and see what happens or continue the medications and recovery treatment plan and know for certain the unfortunate emergency Linda experienced the day before would be repeated. The doctor explained Linda had suffered with Cushing's Disease and after several surgeries (including two pituitary surgeries and an adrenalectomy), Linda was left with Addison's Disease. We all understood the result if the medication was stopped. The body can't survive more than a few days without Cortisol. Linda was prescribed synthetic Cortisol to take for the rest of her life after the adrenal glands were removed.

After a brief conversation among us all in the room, Linda said "I'm sick of being sick. I don't want to be a burden to my family or worry about when this will happen again". It was a decision that was easy for her but would affect me and our daughters in ways we could not imagine. With my approval through my daughters, Linda's decision to stop all treatment spread to friends, family, and neighbors. A few close friends came to visit the hospital to say hello. Even the person who abandoned Linda when she was sick and needed them the most, came to visit.

Eight years ago, Linda went through a manic episode from her Bi-Polar disease. Linda talked to friends and neighbors non-stop for hours if they allowed it. She approached people in stores with no filter and sometimes said rude remarks. Our local grocery store requested I never leave Linda's side and leave when finished shopping. A fifteen-year-old girl in our neighborhood approached Linda with a candy bar and offered it to her; Linda slapped the candy bar away saying she was diabetic, "Are you trying to kill me?" The mother witnessed Linda pushing the candy bar away from the young girl and told Linda never to touch my daughter again. This was a close friend of Linda, and they never spoke again. I had a real problem with the particular visitor who was the last to disappear, now visiting Linda for closure. I needed to hide my emotions and not express my distain for this, so-called friend. As people came to visit, smiles emerged; laughter, and tears were endless.

The first three days went by and Linda was able to eat freely with no regard to diabetic diet restrictions. She called the hospital kitchen on the room phone rattling off a variety of food she wanted, but because of her diabetes, was earlier restricted from eating. Two hospice nurses from two separate companies came to Linda's room sell me their services. One hospice nurse reflected that Linda would go to a house with an open vacancy room all set up for her. I would pay a $3000.00 a month flat fee. Linda would go there until her death. I told the hospice nurse, Linda had only three days left to live. The hospice nurse said the $3000.00 was for the month regardless of one day or thirty days. I visited the house that afternoon and did not find the surroundings inviting at all. I could not find myself sitting in the room or house waiting for the end. That same afternoon another hospice nurse came in with her selling pitch. The cost of hospice care would be $4000.00 and would pay down as the days passed. If Linda passed tomorrow, I would get a refund of the remaining balance $3867.00. I talked with the hospitalist doctor about my dilemma and hated all the options. The doctor said Linda was slipping faster than expected and was too fragile to transfer and would remain in the hospital. I am in medical sales and was appalled by this hospice system and business approach. It was a surreal discussion we were having, planning the last days of Linda's life.

Out of the blue, Linda's mother who lives in Las Vegas called. Linda's doctor asked her mother only to contact Linda in an emergency. Linda and her mother bounce off each other, and Linda was often irrational and hyper after speaking with her parents. Linda's mother did not know or acknowledge the gravity of Linda medical condition but heard from my eldest daughter "My Mom is in the hospital and not doing well." During Linda's conversation with her mother… her mom told Linda to fight for her life and made plans for her to visit them. They told her, "The doctors are wrong." Linda gave the phone to my youngest daughter and said, "My parents don't understand and are driving me nuts". My daughter tried explaining to her grandparents the circumstances of Linda's illness and said everything was tried to help Mom. The grandparents told my daughter, "You're killing your mom." My daughter then gave me the phone and my in-laws yelled at me over the phone "You're killing your wife." I tried explaining the medical emergency three days earlier. They did not want to listen.

Linda complained of pain and the hospice nurse told me and Linda that she would not suffer and asked the hospital nurse for pain medication to be given. Looking back, I was not aware at that time, the pain medications given would put Linda in a deep sleep that she would not wake from. That would be the last conversation I would have with Linda after knowing her for thirty years.

To relax and keep my sanity I decided to take a break. I asked the nurse how long Linda had to live so I could be at her bedside for the end. I was told most likely sometime the next day. Feeling comfortable with that answer, I drove to a small community 20 minutes away and stopped in on a business account. Not normal behavior for someone about to lose their wife and best friend of 30 years, but I needed a sense of stability and normalcy. The cell phone rang with an unidentifiable number. I answered, "Hello…" A moment of silence was on the other end, then a familiar voice said "Mr. Prell?" "Yes" I said. "I'm sorry, your wife passed away." Nothing could have prepared me for that moment…that call. I was shaking, crying, not thinking correctly. I called my brother and told him Linda died. We cried, for who knows how long. I was in a state of shock. Of course, I expected her death, but on my timeline. I should not have been driving at that moment, distracted and all that goes with a lack of focus. My first thoughts were, **I miss Linda. I will never hug, kiss, or hear my wife's voice ever again.** Yes, we had our arguments and disagreements, but over-all I hated her illness and never stopped caring for her. Her illness was not her fault, but it defined her life to others. We are all looking for someone to **share a meaningful and heartfelt hug, a gentle kiss, hold a hand, and have a meaningful conversation.**

I returned to the hospital twenty minutes later to view Linda's body, still warm to the touch and with a peaceful look on her face, not seen in years. Linda was at peace. I clearly remember her words just days earlier, "I'm sick of being sick". She was no longer sick. I held her hand and reflected on what I did to care for her. Initially in those moments I felt a sense of relief or freedom. The stress and weight of ten years living and caring for her and the constant, "What Ifs" slowly lifted off my shoulders and melted away. The what if she was off her meds? What if she started dialing numbers from our address book? What if I could not find a care giver was the most stressful.

In the care giver search, I found friends of my children, who were eighteen to twenty-two; whose parents had told them it is time to leave the house. These were good kids in general, perhaps lacking maturity and responsibility, but still had empathy.

I invited three kids over three years to help with caring for Linda, offering free room and board. My youngest daughter suggested one of her friends at the time. He was willing to do anything: clean the house, cook simple meals, and take Linda to doctor appointments. Overall, he was good company for her. A time came when my tool kit was missing and he admitted to taking it to the family farm to do repairs. But it was never returned. In the big picture, he did as I asked. After a year, he decided to take another direction leaving me on another care giver search. My oldest daughter suggested another friend, who was a restless and seemed a little off his game. Looking back in time I think he too had a chemical imbalance either Bi-Polar or a sort of mood disorder. Perhaps he was homeless at one time because he brought nothing with himself as he moved into our guest room. I did not do a background check on him or ask the typical interview question as all Home Health Agencies do. I was offering a free room for care of my wife and money was tight. He moved in and helped with simple meals and cleaning, while keeping an eye out for Linda. He was quiet most of the time and slept in till 10:00 or 11:00 at times. He worked odd jobs including a sorter at the local dump. He took public transportation that suited him fine. About six months after moving in, my youngest daughter who had her bedroom next to our guest room shared a text message she got from him. "I love you and can't stop thinking about you". I confronted him and asked why he would he sacrifice a good living situation for such a destructive text? He admitted to being off his meds. I gave him three days to move out and insisted he have no contact with my daughter, without me being a witness. My daughter said, she was scared. On reflection, I should have taken him to a homeless shelter. Clearly, he had mental issues and medication adjustment was needed. Letting him stay in our home for extra days was a bad decision.

A few weeks later, my oldest daughter mentioned a girlfriend who lived in an apartment nearby and had a cat she couldn't keep. The cat needed a home. The girl was about 20, well mannered, and a little hyper. Talked fast and not always in common sense terms. You would think by now I would recognize mental illness or troubled youth. I might even have better judgment about my kids' friends, and safety concerns, but to find a caregiver for simple chores and cooking simple meals was priceless and I admit today to having blinders on. I talked to the landlord about this girl and the cat. The landlord was a bit angry, saying the girl owes him back rent and the cat was never allowed. I offered her the guest room and the cat was simply part of the package. I told the landlord, the girl might owe you back rent, but doesn't have a dime to her name. Write it off. My daughter was thrilled to have her friend move in and to get a cat as an extra bonus. To my regret and surprise, my daughter still considers the cat hers to this day, ten years later.

She was, as the others a bit odd in character. She referred to her 'Grammy' often. No talk about parents or other family members. She helped with Linda, and cooked simple meals. She was very protective of her room, by locking it all the time. I know this, because every time she came out of the guest room, I would hear the turn of the lock. One day I picked her up from her Grammy's house, a worn-out mobile home in a depressed mobile home park. My conversation with her Grammy was brief, and she thanked me for taking in her granddaughter and that she'd had a rough up-bringing. Parents and drugs and the sort. The conversation ended abruptly when she came back into the room. She helped out as the others did before her arrival, but there was a bit of a wild side to her of frequent boy guests. I finally put an end to that, which was not received well. She floated an idea to my eldest daughter about moving to Washington. I thought this would be an excellent idea and perhaps allow my daughter to mature. I had a Nissan sedan my daughters drove, not in the best shape, but ran well. She asked if she could buy the car from me. Knowing the difficulty in finding good used cars and a concern about safety, I agreed. Looking back at all my decisions with young kids, money, and the lack of permanent job security all these decisions turned out to be a bad judgement on my part. Shortly after Linda passed away, my daughter, her friend, and her "brother" left in the car for Lynnwood/Brier, WA and I never saw a dime of payment. I felt after Linda was gone it was a good time for my daughter to get away. Months later the car needed new tires because they were never rotated and then an accident that totaled the car.

All the people involved in Linda's care came for a final visit in the hospital. It was bittersweet. I learned the kids mean well, but lack the maturity was a survival instinct.

For the first time in thirty years, I was alone. Ate meals alone, slept alone and the hugs, kisses, holding hands, and of course conversations were missing leaving a huge void. I don't think anyone really thinks about how comfortable we get in a certain lifestyle good or bad. We take the good for granted and hate to admit the bad, really isn't so bad as part of life.

Shortly after Linda passed, possibly months, a young man I met at the cigar lounge called me. He was about twenty-two, very studious (always reading and listening to audio books) and friendly with the younger crowd. He explained he was sleeping on the floor of a friend's apartment and they all decided to leave, leaving him with the apartment abandonment bill. I didn't question his motive, but he asked if he could chill at my house for a few weeks while sorting things out. "Why not", I agreed. Afterall, the house was empty, other than my youngest daughter. Soon after moving in, he started cooking great meals and using the BBQ for ribs and such. He cleaned up after himself and actually helped with house chores. His favorite pass time was listening to and reading audio books, smoking a Hookah while friends came over to party. It actually brought back a sense of normalcy. A bit of my college days was re-lived. He also liked the challenge of school and I was training for a new job.. He asked if he could do the reading and tutor me., something of a game for him. It appears he generally got 98 to 100% on college tests as his friends testified. I agreed and life became a little normal for the first time in years.

To his entertainment, he became part of my dating game. I would meet woman in different circles and circumstances and bring woman home on occasion. He would laugh and ask after the woman left to go home, "Are you serious? You can do better than that...chuckle".

This roommate situation went on for a few years, until he reconnected with his old high school sweet-heart and we all knew, he met his match.

This is my new path to find **hugs, kisses, holding hands** (physical touch) and of course **eye contact and conversations** (non-physical). Initially my book was titled "**I Miss**": Hugs, Kisses, and Conversation". It flowed so smoothly off my tongue. But life does not always flow smoothly, and I realized as I was writing this book and I could not leave out **holding hands and eye contact.** It is a unique chemistry among people that defines a couple and when we allow all these physical and non-physical actions to spontaneously happen. Some friends say I'm looking for love again, aren't we all?

Let's begin with that all important hug. That hug that defines the moment when friends meet again after a long time apart or that first meeting after weeks or months of online chatting. The embrace of genuine caring and connection. I read books in college about non-verbal communications and hugging was well covered and discussed. I also read a phrase on the last page of my final exam in Child Development that for me defines a relationship and stays with me today. **Reading is forgetting, Watching is remembering, and Doing is understanding.** Until you connect with that special person you have not seen in a long time or meet that person who gives genuine hugs, you need to experience that brain rush. The warmth and sincerity of a genuine hug.

So, why bring so much attention to this subject of hugs? It is a defining moment for me when I spend time and energy on a Dating Site communicating with a woman and we agree to meet for the first time. We arrive at that special place, possibly a park or a coffee shop and our eyes meet for the first time. That growing anticipation, our hearts flutter with excitement. We finally connect with a handshake or a **'Grandma / Grandpa hug'** that gentle half-hearted pat on the back instead of a genuine two-arm embrace. Such a let-down, ugh! This is not a genuine embrace, where two arms are extended out and wrap around each other and gently squeeze and this voice whispers in your ear, "It's nice to finally meet you!" or "It's good to see you!" or "Finally, we meet!" The hug is the defining moment when the energy is released. I met several women over the years after Linda passed, and the initial hug and embrace was so important. Unfortunately, it was usually a complete let down. I would reach my arms out and in return I got a gentle pat on the back and or a peck on the cheek. Often it was a limp handshake. Please don't misunderstand me, nothing against the

Grandma's and Grandpa's out in the world. But I suggest after the time and energy you put in to develop a relationship, put a little emotion into your hugs.

I will say, meeting my current wife for the first time and as we departed, she gave me a genuine and sincere tight romantic hug that lasted for a full minute. When she met my children for the first time, she introduced herself with a genuine and sincere hug. My youngest daughter's face transformed in front of my eyes as she melted into her arms. At that moment I said, "This is the one!" Yes, a hug can be that transforming in a relationship. Men out there, remember those hugs in celebration at a sports event, offer that to your children, grandchildren, or woman.

A Kiss is Just a Kiss, don't believe that for a moment. Yes, it appears so simple and sometimes romantic. A non-thinking process, depending on the situation, of two friends, your parents, Grandparents, your children, or lovers. These relationship factors determine how and when a "Kiss" is appropriate. I never felt comfortable kissing my daughters on the lips. I think it was a response one time from my mother-in-law. She saw me kiss my eldest daughter good-bye on the lips, just a friendly peck, and she commented on how wrong and disgusting that was. Looking back at that event, it changed the dynamics of my relationship with my children. I never felt comfortable kissing my children on the lips again. My father-in-law had two daughters; my wife was the youngest of her and her sister. He told me, he kissed his daughters on the lips early on and was scolded the same way by his wife to stop it. Now I can see how family dynamics can alter traditions down the line. Today, I witness fathers in their seventies, kissing their daughters and grandchildren on the lips as a sign of affection and see nothing wrong with it. I was wrong to follow such poor advice years ago.

Sidetracked again. Returning to kissing and romance: I can hear a woman or man saying it now, regardless of your senior age, 'I was kissed on the lips and it felt good!' I have not felt this in so long. Yes, woman can surprise their man too. Remember I mentioned when a woman French kissed me, it took me by surprise. Unfortunately for me, it was not the kiss that turned me off, but more the technique and lack of attraction. Again, going back to brain chemistry. There is a chemical cocktail that is released that can leave you feeling great by igniting the pleasure centers of the brain. The chemicals are oxytocin, dopamine, and serotonin which make you feel euphoric and encourage feelings of affection. Apparently, all the chemicals going off in my brain did not make her look any better in my eyes. That's it for the chemistry lesson. I wanted to make a point here, that it is our subconscious making these decisions.

Kissing is a non-deliberate art. I will also add for our women readers, that flavored and scented lip gloss can change the chemistry of kissing. I remember dating a girl in college and we kissed on occasion. One day, she approached me and put on some cherry scented and flavored lip-gloss. She put her face close to mine as if to whisper something naughty and allowed me to get a scent of her lip-gloss. Then without warning, a full-on kiss. That changed the game for me. As you see, I still have fond memories of that kiss forty years later. No, we are not in college anymore; but if it worked back then, why not today? Women, here is your chance to give your man a zinger he will remember you by for a long time.

"Kiss like you mean it" would be my motto. Ladies and gentlemen, please be prepared for this moment by brushing your teeth, gargle with mouthwash, and have mints or gum handy. A peck on the cheek says as much as a full-on mouth-to-mouth resuscitation kiss. A peck on the cheek says, "Let's be friends".

Holding Hands: Holding hands starts as young as a newborn-- when parents, grandparents, and doctors check for reflex and grip. As we hold out a finger and watch the child reach for and grasp it in a non-thinking reflex. Holding hands is what we do at the end of life as we hold our loved-one's hand, caressing and kissing the hand showing our affection. Holding hands is a sensitive gesture among couples young and old, saying "I care, let's walk through life together", and during a marriage proposal as the man kneels on one knee asking for a woman's hand in marriage. "Stay with me, be with me." I remember my parents walking down the street holding hands and as I mentioned before in the book, they had a "love code". My father would start by gently squeezing my mother's hand, 'Do you love me?' My mother would reply in a returned squeeze 'Yes I do'… My father, 'How much?' And both would squeeze their hands together. Holding hands is a non-thinking gesture. Watch couples as they stroll down a sidewalk or through a store, one partner gently reaches out for the hand of the other. In non-verbal communications it is saying, "be with me because I want to be with you". The man may be holding the partners fingers, a sign of "we are together". Not really a sign of commitment or togetherness. Then, there is the full two hands wrapped together with full ten fingers entangled. It reflects, we are one and I want to be with you. (Friendship with pancaked hands, relationship is waffle hands)

I am guilty of always being in a rush; no reason why. Today, after several years together, I am doing better. She typically reaches out for my hand, and I am genuinely happy to hold her hand with affection. Yes, I need to slow down and learn to be in the moment. The chemistry of hand holding is complex, and I am not going to just fill pages reflecting on details that few people are interested in. Just be aware, we undervalue the importance of hand holding.

Eye contact: "Look into my eyes", we have heard this phrase from Count Dracula, the snake on the Jungle Book, and it is also a song by multiple artists. "Look into my eyes, trust me." The eye gaze is like looking into someone's soul. I could be overplaying this, but have you been asked by a past partner, "What color are my eyes?" and we didn't know? Unfortunately, most people are guilty of this and the answers are deep in research and published studies. After all, we see beauty through our eyes called attraction and everyone sees attraction different. Eye contact is a two-way street: Arousal is elicited by sending and receiving of eye gaze information. Studies show that arousal is enhanced when people make eye contact with a live person compared to viewing a picture of direct or averted gaze. Studies also point toward the potential for social interaction as a possible driving force behind the arousal enhancement. Meaning, eye gaze is not only a signal perceived but also a signal sent out in order to communicate with others. If you are looking for ways to develop a relationship, you have company. While social relationships may come easy to some of us, regardless of the age, like for an extrovert, eye contact may come naturally. As an introvert in our senior years, we are only gazing at another person. I promise, if you look at another person and catch their eye gaze, give them a slight childish eye wink…you will make their day. Perhaps even cause them to blush because you just paid them the highest compliment. How could they not smile back!

Conversations: But I don't know what to say? Where do you start a conversation with any stranger, regardless of how you meet (future) or met (past). The standard who, what, where, when, how, and why is a good start. Yes, again through my homework, I searched communications and was overwhelmed with countless books and published articles on the subject. Communications is really a broad topic, just bringing this subject up in my book is opening up a

Pandora's Box. To simplify this conversation, I brought up in my book "I Miss" Conversation. What did I really miss when conversations ended with Linda and what did I want to replace with the void? Who would or could fill the void? Let's start with extrovert (open to talk and share, not shy) and introvert (not big on talking, and more into listening).

───◆───

If you met on a Dating service, you can't assume everything is as it was presented. Finally meeting in person, is a great way to confirm what the person posted. If you are like me, an extrovert, you like sharing thoughts and even sharing these thoughts out loud. The women I get along with are great listeners and I need to learn to reciprocate. Thus, after writing and reading my work, I Miss the active listener I lived with for thirty years. The partner who was patient enough to actively listen to my rants and offer constructive feedback. My, A-plus extrovert personality does well with an introvert who is good at active listening and enjoys quiet time and reading.

On the other hand, what happens when two extroverts meet? It can be a predictable disaster in the making. Because you think you have a lot in common does not mean it is a good match. Both partners can enjoy sports and competition, but to make it interesting, perhaps it should be different sports for conversations leading to commonality of the sport activity, as well as differences. Women's soccer in Portland, Oregon is big news and so are the Portland Trailblazers basketball team.

What happens when two introverts get together? Personally, I would think boring. But after a conversation with a few couples who are self-proclaimed introverts, they don't have the competitive edge. One couple is composed of a rocket engineer (analytical) and the other partner a teacher (well read). Both enjoy camping in quiet and isolation watching the stars at night.

I met my current wife who is more of an introvert and loves reading. She is an active listener and politely lets me know when she has had enough of my rants. She is an environmental activist at her job and in practice, as we pick up trash on the river left behind from the frequent guests.

Returning to communications and the current lead conversation starter, we can ask each other "Are you in your mind an extrovert or introvert?" "What are your favorite books or movies?" "What are your hobbies?" Conversations are meant to get to know each other, not to be analytical. Conversations I missed were just listening skills on Linda's end and found in my current wife. I am not an easy person to be around. I came with baggage, as we all do in our senior years. This part of the book on I Miss, Conversations could be a thousand pages, but I am not here to just fill pages. Take what you can from hugs, kisses, conversations, holding hands, eye contact and recognize it is a combination of all of them that makes a relationship work.

I MISS

Slow down and be aware of your surroundings in public; I do. I play mind games observing couples and asking what was a deal breaker that may have been put aside or overlooked when a couple first met? Everyone in our senior years come with some baggage. What defines '**Deal breakers**' in relationships? Some deal breakers start as we look at someone in a judgmental way and we don't give a potential relationship a chance to start or blossom. For example: I went to a local bar for first time in many years. I wanted to check out what I was missing out on, since several friends suggested I go to a bar, grab a simple drink, and just chill. I took their advice, wondering what type of woman I would meet. I was sipping an iced tea, not exactly a bar drink and a woman caught my eye. She was about my age, with long blond hair, and a nice figure. I walked over to her and introduced myself and just started a conversation. As she drank her bottle of beer, sip after sip our conversation flowed and beer breath soon lingered in the air. She soon finished the bottle and asked the bartender for another. We talked for about a half hour, and soon she started slurring her words. As the conversation dragged on, she started to paw at my leg. She asked me if I lived close by. I suggested she had enough, and no I did not live close. I excused myself and said I was going to the bathroom and I walked out the back door.

Looking back at this event, it was an awkward time for me. I was never a bar personality to begin with and don't care for people who don't know their alcohol limit. I should keep moderation in mind since many people drink socially. I was anxious to have feelings again no matter the source. However, as judgmental as it may appear, bars are not in my comfort zone. I was trying the bar crowd, because …You guessed it, **I Missed** hugs, kisses, holding hands, and conversation. I did not consider a simple conversation with women flirting, after all it is just a simple conversation. However, my daughters saw me talking to women as flirting.

It is now time to live again, no matter how you found yourself single or available. The words you use to describe your marital status really does not matter to others. Single does not equate to lonely. In my experience, lonely is a state of mind. I'm not going to get into the nuances on the psychology of loneliness, but I can't remember being lonely. I looked up loneliness on the internet and found volumes of books and published articles relating to loneliness. The same amount of information was available when I looked up grieving. Getting sidetracked again, but after a closer look, I would warn us all that we make poor decisions and choices when we are drunk or lonely looking for a partner or significant other.

This applies equally to men and women. I believe we make impulsive decisions when we are not thinking in the right mindset. Again, it is complicated and simply said, ask yourself if the person you just met is lonely, grieving or…fill in the blanks? Fit the question into a conversation. Perhaps that will be your connection. However, as a conversation starter, I am not sure I would want to have a long conversation about each other's loneliness or grieving. Then again, the conversation may expose a deal breaker?

Getting back to deal makers and breakers as mentioned earlier; I want to have fun with this and not take it so seriously. Think of this as an SNL skit. List deal breakers that would turn you off. Then, make a separate list of what would be 'Deal Makers' that would turn you on? I found 'Deal Breakers' more entertaining. Afterall, when I viewed profiles on Dating apps, after the picture I often read: "No hook-ups, no smokers or active addicts".

Deal Breakers

For me (a man): You can choose three for fun or just make up your own. Have fun with this exercise.

I don't care for short hair. But if I was dating a woman with long hair and she suddenly cut it for the summer heat, I would not fault her. Men at our age are not that shallow or insensitive.

Heavy make-up is a turn off for me. Make-up was intended to highlight the face, not cover it up. Simply said, if it takes a woman over a half hour to put on makeup for work or to go out for the evening, she is not my type. I do understand and respect that this ritual is typically done for our behalf. Don't take offense women, there are plenty of men that appreciate this ritual. My current wife, for example, will ask me if I would like her to put on makeup for a night on the town?

Old tattoos and face jewelry: I may be old fashioned, but old and faded tattoos and face jewelry tell me a story of an impulsive personality. It tells me that at one time, this person made a decision that will be forever on their body. They were either drunk, bowed to peer pressure, or this tattoo is a constant reminder of a very important time in their life they never want to forget. Sometimes I wonder if that impulsive decision making carried over into their senior years.

There are people who will insist, since I don't have tattoos, that I have no right to judge. This is a true, however I find people who get tattoos as a bold statement or for a very important memory. I want to know the history behind this courageous decision. Yes, technology has come a long way and this body art is intended to last a lifetime looking good. Body art conferences are well attended and many people find tattoos attractive and even sexy. Thus, a **deal maker** for many people would be to find a future partner at a body art festival. Even those with nose rings, ear loop gages, tongue piercings, cheek drops, lip rings and such. There is a partner for everyone.

———◆———

Alcohol in general: I think I covered my thoughts about drinking in detail earlier. I personally don't care for alcohol breath or for people who don't know their limit. But I recognize this is a selected group and I am not against having fun and enjoying the fruits of our community. I know wine tasting is popular in my community, along with beer pubs. Wine enthusiasts travel to vineyards tasting wines from around the country and even the world. Equally popular is beer tasting. I attended a wine tasting here and there over the years and watch as the tasting begins and the laughing and smiles grow. People having a great time, and then they drive off in a vehicle. I don't mean to be a "kill joy", I understand it is selective on my part; these people having fun trying wines and tasting beers, but I find it a turn off in my dating life. I did find a partner who does not drink, or at least on the rare occasion when she does drink, it is one glass. But again, if you like wine and beer as a

Deal maker: I would think a wine tasting event or beer festival a great way to meet that special person.

Deep faith: OK, now I am going to lose some fans. Mind you, it is my belief: everything in moderation. It's great when people wear a pendant reflecting their faith, but a large pendent cross is too much for me. It might be the greatest sign of strength and attraction for many people looking for a partner. I am sure they can start a conversation. I grew up in a Jewish community and yes, woman wore the Star of David on a pendent, but the jewelry was small and not screaming out "I'm Jewish".

Tobacco products: This is definitely where I can predict you calling me a hypocrite. I can play both sides of this argument. I find women smoking cigarettes disgusting. The habit is an addiction, a long and bad addiction at this stage in our lives. It tells me this person has an addictive personality and potentially life- threatening health issues currently or possibly in the near future. Cigarettes leave behind an odor on your breath, hands, and clothes. Years of smoking will stain teeth and is horrible for gum disease. Your skin ages faster with tobacco products and that soft skin men like to caress is not so soft. Enough said about cigarettes, but yes, I like my cigars and I tell my partners I smoke cigars. Some women tell me outright cigars are disgusting and I am OK with that. I do respect that cigars are synonymous with bad breath, smelly clothes, and a lingering odor in the hair and air. However, some cigars do actually smell good, taste great during a kiss, and have a social calling.

My current wife made me a man cave on our back deck with cigar accessories and all for me to host cigar events. She actually likes the smell of a couple specialty cigars. I have met intelligent and on business level, very helpful men and women who enjoy the art of cigars. OK, now I am not being fair, romancing cigars over cigarettes. But in fairness, cigars are not inhaled. They do have a following among the elite. I will say on the women's behalf, guys in selective groups love chew. Guys take that pinch from the can and put it in their cheek, let the saliva build up in their mouth and as the saliva drools out of their mouth, then they spit. Really guys, in front of their women. To my surprise, especially in the mid-west ranches, women just accept it as part of the culture. I can't imagine a woman kissing a man after spitting out chew with the stained teeth and tobacco breath. This is really fun to write. I can picture the women reading this and laughing, saying "Yep, that's my man!" I can also picture a few men reading this and saying, "Really, that's all you got?" Deal breakers really are more a test of tolerance. What is it that is truly "me" that others will accept, and I can live with their perceived faults too?

Narrow minded thinker: This is a person who it appears was raised in a culture and can't see the beauty in others. I like educated people and can see religion, politics, body images, and such clouding judgement. Narrow minded thinking could be a book in its own right. "I don't like," fill in the gaps… liberals, conservatives, fat, thin. It is endless.

My wife is a BBW (Big Beautiful Woman) and identifies as a Christian. In her car alone, she listens to contemporary Christian music. I am a thin, older Jewish man and I listen to 70's rock and medical talk shows. I would not call myself narrow minded.

Mental illness: Yes, I will get feedback loud and clear for my thinking. I experienced mental illness first-hand and feel I have a voice. Without getting into too much detail, mental illness is a broad subject and effects people in so many different ways. My first impression would be to avoid getting close and avoid building a relationship. If I was thinking of getting involved with a person as a partner again, I would want to hear and understand their medical history with mental illness and how fragile they are. Meaning, how often they have breakthroughs of mania or depression and/or other afflicting chemical imbalances. Through a sensitive and adult conversation, I would ask if they were ever hospitalized and I would like to know the medication they are taking. In brief, at this stage in my life (60's) I would avoid a new partner with mental illness. This is because, as we age, mental illness becomes more unpredictable or fragile. Medication for brain chemical imbalance is expensive on a limited income and titration up and down is tricky. Therapy is a life journey and family should actively participate.

Intimacy or Hookups: The 60's and 70's was a great time with the free love movement, but the ultimate turn-off "Deal Breaker" for a woman in her senior years is the perceived hook-up approach by men. We are not teenagers anymore with out-of-control hormones. Let me revisit that statement: the reason women don't have the same drive as men in the senior years is a result of hormone changes. Men are helped along at this age with Cialis and Viagra. But, without these boosters for arousal, men would not have these feelings either. So, I suggest taking the romance slow and have a conversation about intimacy.

Oh, I'm just getting started. No wonder I stayed single for so long.

Deal Makers:

Unlike "Deal Breakers", some people may look at this list as "negative thinking", while I look at both Deal Makers and Deal Breakers as simply entertaining. **Deal Makers** is just another way to see people for what you are **attracted to**. It can be a fun and entertaining exercise to do alone, with a friend, or a group of friends. Have fun and create a social event. In my opinion, Deal Breakers are more fun to do list. Again, Deal Makers are a list of characteristics of a future partner that I or "you" would find as a "**turn on**", so to speak. Some people could say "Deal Makers" are just the opposite of Deal Breakers. Possibly, but picture yourself on a two-way round trip sight-seeing train to and from a destination sitting in the same seat viewing the same landscape. Seeing the scenic ride in a different perspective to and from is similar to viewing a partner with Deal Makers and Deal Breakers. Deal Breakers in reality are not black and white, and at our age, there is typically a lot of grey (no pun intended).

My **Deal Makers** in part are:

I like a woman with long hair (color aside) as said earlier. I like to see and feel long hair on woman as I run my hands through and along the edges. This Deal Maker can apply to women too, who may look for a man with the long hair of the "Rock Star" image. In the age group my book refers to, women commonly cut and style their hair for simplicity. No more long and unkempt hair for the grandchildren to grab a hold of with sticky fingers. Less time washing long hair and the burden of conditioners and other hair products. In our age group, for both men and women, hair goes through hormone stages and changes, regardless of the hair preparations we use and try to save what we can. Hair becomes thinner, less bulky and becomes brittle. Let's face it guys, we completely lose our hair or the famous receding hairline and ponytail. Age plays a role on the health of hair in both men and women.

Makeup: is in the gray zone and can be a Deal Maker or Deal Breaker. Properly applied, makeup can take years off a woman's age. My mother had a simple makeup collection on a ten-inch sterling silver tray on her dresser, passed down to her by her mother. This sterling silver tray and makeup collection remained with her on the same dresser on the day of her passing. The dresser and tray are with me today as a warm reminder of my grandmother and mother. My mother (in the seventies) gently applied just a bit of rouge to the cheeks, a dash of eye accent, and lightly applied lip-gloss for special evenings out. Growing up with this image is why heavy makeup is on my deal breaker list, but properly applied makeup is on my deal maker list. There are no hard rules to follow in my book, just have fun with your friends and share stories.

A Great listener: is such a turn on for both men and women. It shows "we care". Listening skills are sympathizing with your partner and understanding the emotional rollercoaster we all ride. I can't tell you how many times I have heard "you don't know me" or "you never listen". Listen please, both men and women should take a class in communications with a focus on listening skills. Honestly, I am the worst listener and recognize my weakness. Have fun with your partner and play the Dating Game in a romantic setting next to a fire with a glass of wine. What are favorite foods, favorite music, memorable places, movies, and TV shows? You will immediately know who the listener is.

Faith: Is a huge Deal Maker for millions of people. Often, faith is the first item listed on Dating services as the Deal Maker. Faith is also mentioned as the Deal Breaker, "Don't contact me if you don't have a relationship with Jesus". This is not my specialty as a Reformed Jewish man leaning toward Agnostic. It is a personal choice and fact that people turn to faith, regardless of what religion it is to help themselves through hard times. Attempting to understand the people who go to Dating apps "especially the men" for a future partner, it appears hypocritical to me to read about deep faith on a Dating app profile. I am walking a tight rope again. Having a commitment to faith while sharing life experiences and listening skills could play a major role in conversations.

Good Health: Nothing is more of a **Deal Maker** than good health and hygiene. Feeling good about yourself. A clean body, clean healthy hair, fresh breath, and just looking healthy. "I care about myself and I certainly want to care about you." Oh, I could and might go on for pages with Deal Makers, and it is so much fun to find that special someone with the attraction and characteristics that say, "YES, tell me more about you".

Deal Makers and Deal Breakers for Women

Deal Breakers and Deal Makers for Women: Choose three just for fun or make up your own.

Deal Breakers: Men or partners who are rude, sarcastic, beer breath, smoke cigarettes, bad language, shallow minded, tattoos, facial jewelry, nose picking, facial stubble, hygiene, financial struggles, and strong politics.

An example of **how to play Deal Breakers** or to take a positive spin on this is **Deal Makers**:

I was driving along a rural highway in my small town where I live and saw large flower baskets hanging from a medal frame as I passed by a nursery. I stopped in to briefly look at the flower basket collection. I watched as a woman was checking out the baskets too, as she was reaching up trying to take a hanging basket down. From first glance, she was wearing heavy makeup (**deal breaker**), tight designer jeans (**a deal maker**), and clean tennis shoes. I offered to help her get the basket down, and she replied, "I am fine". In a brief conversation, she said "It is hard to see all the flowers from looking up and I like to check soil temperature and moisture". In other words, were the flower baskets healthy or just for show not to last long after a purchase? In my experience, she was not a person I would be interested in pursuing. We both liked being outdoors (**deal maker**) but, she did not appear to be a person who likes to get dirty (**deal breaker**), a negative for me. She wore high-fashion clothes and did not feel comfortable in public without heavy makeup (**deal breaker**). I realize I appear very picky, but it is an example of how I think. I am usually aware of the people around me and wondering in the back of my mind who they really are.

I know plenty of men who would have thought this woman would be a person to pursue or a (**deal maker**). They would have seen this woman as well educated about her hobbies (**deal maker**), presents herself with confidence in public (**deal maker**), bit sassy and can hold her own. Only way to know is to strike up a conversation. I can touch on conversation starters later in the book. Conversation starters would also depend on if the first contact is on-line "dating app", phone, or in person.

Another example I thought of is meeting a person of interest at a rodeo, especially in the Northwest or Mid-West. The women (**deal breakers**) might be the men are often loud, drinking a lot of beer, cussing, chewing tobacco…need I go on. The women (**deal makers**) could be the men are strong, the men are brave, men are committed to their craft.

Men (**deal makers**) at a rodeo are woman often dress in form fitting jeans, like beer, and are typically attending to find a man, similar to a dating app. Honestly, can't really think of men **deal breakers** for woman at a rodeo.

I asked my girlfriend at the time, now my current wife, if women see or look at men in public places the same way men look at woman. She said, emphatically no. "Women have a purpose or a mission when they are shopping. They just go about their business." She added, "Men are pigs…. always looking for sex…to get laid." What are your thoughts reading this, both men and women can chime in on this discussion? Yes, a funny and out of this world question. What I am saying is that we make judgments about people. We all have our unintended bias.

The Deal Breaker game is just that, a fun puzzle with no science to support the facts. But I firmly believe, **our brain chemistry drives our Deal Makers and Deal Breakers**.

I am attracted to woman with long blond or brunette hair, well endowed (call it what you're most comfortable with), and a chunky body style or overweight. My first wife, Linda, had brown hair, smaller cup size, and an average to chunky build. Looking back at high school days, my high school girlfriend had blond hair, a large front porch, and was overweight.

Thus, I pose the question to the women? In high school, were you attracted to the science nerd or the jock? I am stereo typing now, I am aware. Fast forward to your fifties, sixties, and seventies, what are your deal breakers today? This question is posed to both men and women. Is thinning hair on men or woman effect your attraction? Perhaps you have accepted the beer belly or perhaps poor dental hygiene? We all compromise and personally, I never liked heavy makeup on woman. This is true today as it was in high school, probably stemming from the women in my family.

Social media

What is meant by social media, you ask? What we are exposed to everyday by news headlines, television, and the internet. The media exposes us to celebrities who are no different than you and I. They could be divorced, widowed or widower. I see a celebrity who has fought weight balance issues for years taking lead on Weight Watchers, now renamed WW. Renamed to fight the weight "name" and to rethink the public persona of fat people. Now WW is to mean Health and Wellness, not just shedding pounds. Weight Watchers built a successful reputation on losing weight, and now to broaden its audience appeal is refocusing on nutrition. I think this is great, but it started with obesity as its focus. Queen Latifa is a BBW (big, beautiful woman) and a successful artist and actor. Plenty of head shots on her new series, no body camera shots. Then there is "My Big Fat Fabulous Life" and Honey Boo Boo. Enough said, you get the idea. In the male image, we can't forget Edie Murphy as Professor Klump in the Nutty Professor or Fat Albert. The social media has amplified size of a person to be a comedy.

There are examples of normalcy, but we understand, when someone says, she is dating the Nutty Professor. It works both ways. I am not saying I have an answer to this social media frenzy on body image, but I do think it reflects on who we see and how we perceive them. On the television show Mike and Molly, a show about a plus size couple, the show reflected how there is someone for everyone. Yes, even overweight people. The character Molly it is said in the media was losing weight for health reasons and supported by the medical community. The show's producers threatened to cancel her contract as it was not the character image they had hired her for.

◆

Dating Sites and Services

It is time to inject a little humor. Three months after Linda passed away; I started dating again experimenting with dating sites. I would not highly recommend this as a starting point now that I have some experience with this social medium. If you look at dating sights or 'services" as a bit of entertainment and don't take them too seriously, they are actually fun and can be seen as "The Dating Game". You can ask yourself, who might I be attracted to or who might I find common interests with? But as most dating sight profiles suggest, people say they are looking for "long term relationships" or suggest from a woman's point of view 'no hook-ups', meaning I'm not interested in a one-night stand. Of course, unless you might be the "one".

I was simply missing hugs, kisses, and holding hands at the time, thus, dating sights were the easiest way to connect at the time with a potential future partner. I discovered most people take these services way too serious. Conversations are important as discussed throughout my book, but a new beginning starts with the physical touch. Allison Kraus recorded a song, 'You Say it Best when you Say Nothing at All'. The song speaks volumes to touch and eye contact. Non-physical touch such as eye contact and conversations follow closely. In fact; I will call myself out on this. Many people meet and are first attracted to the eye contact. The chemistry that happens when you first make eye contact makes us feel good and connects us. I remember dancing at a Disco in the seventies and asking my dates to look at me while we were dancing. I would tell my dancing partner 'The Eyes tell no Lies', I know it sounds a bit corny, it's true. Prolonged eye contact, it is said through numerous studies has been thought to release phenylethylamine, a chemical responsible for feelings of attraction. It has also been thought to release oxytocin, the love chemical most closely associated with longer term bonding and commitment.

I can't honestly say, I remember looking into Linda's eyes for the commitment of love. I was more into the hugs, kisses, and holding hands. Moving forward, I think my Deal Makers as mentioned before are growing and I will be more aware of eye contact. I will be testing if I get my heart fluttering after making eye contact with an attractive woman.

To my point, people will negatively comment about me using Dating Services shortly following Linda's death. I'm aware there are "services" to provide us with the physical touch; talking about walking a politically correct tightrope. I am not shy; I guess you could call me an extrovert. In most cases, I feel comfortable introducing myself to strangers depending on the situation and environment. I can strike up a conversation, but quickly find myself bored if I don't hear some commonality to tie us together to maintain the conversation flow. I can connect with the song by Rod Stewart: "Every Picture Tells a Story don't it". In my experience; every person has a story, don't they?

I find dating has not changed much over the years. I'm not in college anymore, so to transition into dating slowly I became a member of several online dating sites, more for entertainment than to meet the woman or partner of my dreams.

Using Google to search dating sights for 50+ singles will reveal several Apps to choose from, even rated in order of popularity. But I caution you; the information requested initially from these dating sites appears harmless, it can lead to massive computer solicitation. I was asked for my email address and how close in location do I want these potential partners? I recognize now that they have my zip code? The requested information on several of the dating sites asks for my credit card number to bill me after the first free month, trial. I suggest taking a long pause before giving any personal or credit card information. I can hear the reader now saying, of course I wouldn't just give my personal information. But our minds tend to wander and people think, what if it works? It can't hurt to try? I'm sick of being alone… what the heck, why not? That was my attitude when I signed up for my first Dating app and found it very difficult to cancel the dating app subscription. I discovered that this was not the way to find my next true love. I called Dating app company customer service I found on Google, e- mailed the company and looked for an address. Eventually, I called my credit card company to cancel a dating app subscription payment. I discovered the company was charging my credit card for several months after I canceled and I had already deleted the App from my phone. If you check your credit card statement in detail monthly, you can avoid this potential problem. I found the same people on several Dating sites looking for a partner. I would consult friends or family members who also used dating apps and ask what their experience is or was and what their favorite is? If they found one that they liked, then subscribe to that one for a month. Save some money and play the Dating Game with fun in mind. loneliness is an opportunity for big business and Dating app developers know this. One month subscription leads to three months, and to six months, and you are hooked.

Moving forward, you decided to go for it and try a subscription. I have talked with several people who have met "Online" and find this is a broad term. On a typical dating site people list faith, hobbies, career, and frequently the 'Deal Breakers" first followed by the "Deal Makers", described in detail later in the book. I especially am amazed when I read from a woman's profile; 'not interested in Hook ups", but one- night stands were popular in the seventies? I guess we all grew up and realized we are not eighteen anymore. These are the same women that grew up looking for 'Hook ups' then. We simply justified it by calling it "free sex", the hippy generation. It was fun to have a brief fling with no strings attached. Couples got married, yet with consensual agreement believed in an "Open Marriage", sharing partners. Seemed simple then, today does it really change the meaning? I also read on women's dating site profiles, "looking for long term relationship". To be fair to both sides; most men who are widowers or divorced and the repercussions from a divorce, are not looking for a long -term relationship. In most cases, men are looking for a 'one night stand' and women for stability.

Let's review and give an example of a traditional Dating Site after you signed up and spent an hour filling in your profile data. When you open the Dating site, it is already set to your preference. Man or woman, you see a picture of the person, the person's profile name and age. Possibly a line regarding education, followed by a section called Looking for, Deal Makers? Their location with a zip code, height, occupation. I am at this time simplifying the person's profile. Unfortunately, most woman and men don't get beyond the pictures and swipe right "I'm interested" or left "NOT". This is the growing model for dating apps. There are several dating Sites with a different format, but I found most Apps have the same people as mentioned before. It's a shallow world of look and swipe. Thus, as suggested I would not put too much energy into this activity, and just have fun entertaining yourself.

What I found myself missing, was and is right in front of us all.

Just living life is the most common way to meet our future sole mate, best friend, lover, significant other…call the person what you want. As I mentioned earlier, I see myself as an extrovert, and meeting people comes easy. When I am in public places, airports, bus stations, coffee shops, the list is endless I ask myself about the people I am seeing and observing.

The book, Blink by Malcom Gladwell explains in detail the mind connection process that happens in a blink of an eye. The book can change the way of thinking about people and dating. The book reflects that we all make some of our most important decisions in a blink of an eye. This way of thinking goes back to the brain chemistry, as a non-thinking process. It's easier to just follow our gut instinct about some issues we face in life. I was aware when I saw the profile of a woman on a random online Dating Site, a smile or something about the woman would catch my eye. I would encourage a text or e mail exchange and then encourage a texting conversation. Following several texts, I would encourage a phone call. Rather childish and almost predatory when I look back at it now. All of the women I connected with refused my request for a phone call, thinking their number would show on my phone and that they might be stalked. I don't think a man would respond the same if a woman asked for his number. I admit if I had a phone conversation I would be listening for clues of intelligence. For the woman I connected with by text, I asked where she lived, what they did for a living, and about financial status? Among other information that would eventually be discovered during a date. I filtered out my 'deal Breakers".

I found to my surprise the book 'Blink' was easily applied when I met the women for the first time. When I met women who are Grandmothers, I got an initially half-hearted grandma hug and peck on the cheek kiss, I felt so turned off. A friend told me, I should never expect a sincere hug or kiss on the first meeting or date. Personally, I disagree. I have found that women who are in a neutering role give very pleasant and sincere hugs and affectionate kisses upon first greetings. It is a trusting gesture that perhaps is difficult to put into words. A genuine hug is a tight and full embrace and trusting gesture. It is also met with a warm smile and genuine simple kiss. Don't get me wrong, I'm not talking about a make out session during a first meeting, but I admit it has been described by many women as "the chemistry, I know it when I feel it". It is not love or lust, but a feeling of trust.

Hugs, kisses, and holding hands can be testing grounds for how a first date went for both men and woman. I have received a genuine hug and sincere kiss at the start of a date and ended several hours later with a grandma's hug and peck on the cheek. This was a clear indication that the date was fun, but not worth a repeat performance. However, I have also experienced a very nice and sincere passionate hug and warm and affectionate kiss and a thank you at the end of a date and thank you for a great time.

Related to Dating sites and services; the advice given to me by a married woman friend was, "if the chemistry is there, I'm going to be tested. A woman is looking forward to the passion the same as the man is". It is a two-way street; an educated woman is looking for similar in an educated man along with trust and sincerity. Not a one-night stand. In short, men need to decide if they want a long-term relationship with a quality partner or a one-night stand. The term "Wham Bam, thank you mam" from the seventies applies here. Free love with no strings attached. The insincere "grandma hug and kiss" is a leery woman who has dated several men and has been burned many times. This is often when I get the Grandma hug and kiss in the beginning and the end of a date. I am told by my friends, be aware of the grandma hug in the beginning of the date and the warm, relaxed, strong affectionate embrace at the end of the date. I may have done something right.

Yes, Blink has opened my eyes to first impressions at a moment's notice. Don't overthink it and allow the natural chemistry to happen. In my experience, the email or texting conversation, turned to phone call, and eventual in person date is a lengthy path, but has led me to no long-term relationships.

Deal Breakers

Dating In college I had what I called "deal breakers", or what I was not looking for in a girlfriend. Very surface minded thinking, and immature. In my mind, the "first date" was more of a meeting. At the time I was looking for a girl who was smart, smarter than me anyway. I am not talking about a master's degree or PhD, but a girl who could have a conversation of current events. Fast forward thirty years, and my deal breakers remain the same. I don't consider my surface minded or immature anymore, just think a smart woman is sexy. It is amazing how time or age changes nothing, and yet everything. My standards for dating were high in college, perhaps too high to override my weaknesses or possible insecurities. Today as a widower, I am still searching for similar qualities in partners as I did in college, but the Deal Breakers list had expanded. It is amazing how a good conversation on local or national events can generate a provocative conversation. In my college years I wanted someone attractive, who doesn't? Of course, this is very subjective. I was looking for a girl who had a job and savings in the bank. I did not smoke or drink, I suppose a nerd at heart. Thus, in college this was a challenge for me. Young and dumb, I was not looking for a wife, but to have fun.

On a Sunday afternoon, back in 1984, my cousin called me to attend a Jewish dance that night at a local Synagogue. I don't dance and had laryngitis from a cold. I did not want to go to this dance. Oh yes; I forgot to mention, I am of Reform Jewish upbringing and did not actively practice my faith then and don't today. But my cousin was far more active in the Jewish community and is still today. I mention this, because this is why my cousin offered the invitation to attend the Jewish dance that Sunday evening. I met my first wife at the dance I attended, to find out later in our relationship she had mental illness. My point in mentioning these details now is to say... Today; I would not have attended a Jewish dance. I would have separated ties "broken-up" with a woman revealing she had mental illness. It is unfortunately true, if I had been firm to the Deal Breakers of that time in college, my current family would not exist. Hindsight is 20/20 and everything happens for a reason, a motto I followed in college and today. I stopped asking why and just accept there is a reason I meet who I am attracted to.

People can ask; and rightfully so, why Deal Breakers? Why can't you just say, "I am looking for" and be done with it? It was and is entertainment for me, a fun game of sorts. What are your Deal Breakers just suggests a conversation. I have a short list of questions I can ask friends or observe in people that explains a mindset. It is easier for me to find out what I am not attracted to than to go out on a date over a period of time and find out through experience what "drives me crazy. I agree, sometimes the experience is half the fun. To support my way of thinking, when you explore the Dating Services, it is often mentioned on a Women's profile under Looking For? It is said, "Don't contact me if you don't follow Christ. Don't contact me if you just want a hook-up. Don't contact me if?" I think you got the idea.

Back in college I did not drink...why you ask? I did not like the taste of alcohol; it is an acquired taste. I worked in an ER as an emergency medical technician and found drinking often leads to getting drunk. Not in all cases, but often in a party setting. I noticed working in the ER on weekends the young people who got into car accidents and other injuries that occurred from stupid acts involving alcohol. Need I say more. Attitudes also change when people get drunk. Dating today, I have been observing social dating sites and looking for "social drinker" or a non-drinker. I really want to prove myself wrong and accept the fact that people drink, and sometimes don't understand limitations. I want to prove to myself; I am over-reacting, and this deal breaker of "non-drinker" or social drinker is ridiculous. Later when I share with you, my humorous dating stories…several women have gotten down right hammered, drunk, call it what you want. Embarrassing for all involved. To my surprise, my deal breakers do end up back firing on me and canceling each other out. I am not religious at all. Most women who don't drink, are very religious. Oh well…drinking will need to be tolerated. Yes, you can laugh now.

My Deal Breakers are: Can't live in a bad neighborhood. Can't be on several anti-psychotic medications (referring to severe mental illness), can't have an empty bank account, can't be more than a social drinker, can't smoke cigarettes, can't be a bible thumper, can't have more than two children (too many grandchildren to spread time around with), can't be into heavy makeup, must tolerate cigars. Can't be unattractive in my eyes, but beauty is in the eye of the beholder, and we all see things differently. Yes, I am partially joking about all of this to prove a point. It is so easy to say what we don't like or want. Then our eyes catch a gaze, she or he is looking back, the heart starts pitter-patter and the brain takes over.

Deal Makers: Must be attractive in my eyes. Must be willing to give sincere hugs, kisses, and hold my hand. A conversation now and then to keep engagement. Must be smart and have a career or income stream. Must want to take care of themselves. Must like the coast. Honestly, I'm not a fan of several children and grandchildren. I have been told, I come after parents, children, grandchildren, and the pets. You get the idea by now.

Circumstances We Meet Under

I find the circumstances of how couples meet and the choice of the first meeting or first date to be as interesting as the chemistry of attraction. The initial connection or 'meeting' can be from an **on-line** dating site, a **coffee shop**, an **outdoor** activity, a **local bar** says a lot about the individuals and the conversation they may have to start the conversation.

Online Dating Sites and Social Media

For fun and not to be taken to serious, I searched and joined several online dating services when I was younger. I repeated the same pattern after Linda passed away for the same reason, just wondering who was available for hugs, kisses, and holding hands on romantic walks. For reasons I still don't completely understand, society frowns on dating services, although it is a billion-dollar industry. Society, when I think about it, actually makes fun of the dating services and of those who participate in the offerings. It can be a little embarrassing to admit to friends or family members, you have a subscription to a dating service.

Personally, I turned that thinking around by sharing the dating app with my friends at a local cigar lounge. We had fun looking at profiles of woman on the dating site and we played around with who we thought would be a good fit for me. Men and woman can actually have fun playing with the dating services and look at this as an opportunity instead of an embarrassment. I understand there is a stigma referring to dating overall in our later years. Then, add into a conversation with close family and friends; "Oh Yeah, and I'm on this dating site." The typical reply is generally, "Oh Really?" with a Garfield the cat grin. The reality is as stated above, dating sites are a popular world-wide billion-dollar industry and there is a reason for this. There is a senior population who are looking for a partner to share life experiences with, no shame needed today. In fact; even though I am working on this book focused on the senior population, what age do you define as senior? Dating services market to a wide range of ages and circumstances. Widowers, Widows, Divorced, and a high travel population, I am sure I'm missing a sub population somewhere.

Prices on dating services range from free to thousands of dollars to help you find the best match or partner. The most expensive dating services can charge up to several thousand dollars promising a safer experience and to avoid the pitfalls offered by other less expensive services. In my experience, I found the other less expensive dating services more reasonable in price and a fun game.

A word to the wise, I would be cautious about giving any personal credit card or billing information to any on-line App or Dating service until I checked out the service online and read some posted reviews. Using Google to search dating sights for 50+ singles will reveal several Apps to choose from, even rated in order of popularity. But I caution you; the information requested initially from these dating sites appears harmless, it can lead to massive computer solicitation. I was asked for my email address and how close in location do I want these potential partners? I recognize now that they have my zip code? The requested information on several of the dating sites asks for my credit card number to bill me after the first free month, trial. I suggest taking a long pause before giving any personal or credit card information. I can hear the reader now saying, of course I wouldn't just give my personal information. But our minds tend to wander and people think, what if it works? It can't hurt to try? I'm sick of being alone... what the heck, why not? That was my attitude when I signed up for my first dating app and found it very difficult to cancel the dating app subscription. I discovered that this was not the way to find my next true love. I called the dating app company customer service I found on Google, emailed the company, and looked for an address. Eventually, I called my credit card company to cancel a dating app subscription payment. I discovered the company was charging my credit card for several months after I canceled and I had already deleted the App from my phone. I if you check your credit card statement in detail monthly, you can avoid this potential problem. I found the same people on several dating sites looking for a partner. I would consult friends or family members who also used dating apps and ask what their experience is or was and what their favorite is? if they found one that they liked, then subscribe to that one for a month. Save some money and play the Dating Game with fun in mind. loneliness is an opportunity for big business and dating app developers know this. One month subscription leads to three months, and to six months, and you are hooked.

Using Google as a search engine, I found Senior 50 Plus dating apps in a preferred order of dating friendly and customer friendly. I also found dating in this population, woman in general want to keep the relationship platonic at first.

There are several Dating Sites to choose from with themes related to age, religion, culture, distance, and long -term relationships versus a one-night fling. Now I need to be careful and keep this subject PG. The list for Deal Makers or Deal Breakers only grows and is endless. I will offer a surface view of what I found searching for a dating app and share an example or two. Endless articles have been written about dating sites and it is intended to be a chemistry of connecting people with likes and dislikes more than an out-rite business. The dating sites

I used are intended for long term relationships rather than a quick meet-up with little interest in for long term romance. This is also indicated in the profile post of most dating service members. For example, I have read on individual profiles: "If you are looking for a 'hook up'... move on"! The fact remains, men and woman are wired different, but with similar brain chemistry. I am not going to get too complex in the understanding of love and brain chemistry but found the simplified version of interest. Richard Schwartz and Jacqueline Olds found in their study of MRI brain scans of college students, brain regions become active with Dopamine, the so-called feel-good neurotransmitter. Two of the brain regions that showed activity in the MRI scans were the caudate nucleus, a region associated with reward detection and expectation and the integration of sensory experiences into social behavior, and the ventral tegmental area, which is associated with pleasure, focused attention, and the motivation to pursue and acquire rewards. All this is really means for me and you in short is, that we really don't make the decisions about who we are interested in pursuing, our brain makes that decision. From a personality view, woman I find in general are looking for a partner who is honest, security, friendship and of course...genuine hugs, gentle kisses, and smart conversation over time. Looks or attraction for woman is not the number one decision maker or Deal Breaker as a theme I have injected into this book.

Men on the other hand, are more visual and don't always think or agree with the "over time" clause or the attraction decision maker. According to Physical attractiveness, Wikipedia facial symmetry is shown to be 'attractive in woman' full lips, high forehead, broad face, small chin, small nose, short and narrow jaw, high cheekbones, clear and smooth skin, and wide set eyes. Personally, I can't see this in my description of what I am looking for. Who are we to question Wikipedia? I guess, I'm wired wrong.

To start, the Dating Service will ask several questions in multiple sections to fill out to who you are? Age, culture, travel, work related hints. Likes and dislikes: Likes for example "hobbies" and dislikes "deal breakers". In the question - answer sections, I was brief. I like fine cigars and don't drink. Thus, a person who has asthma and likes wine tasting will pass on choosing me. Depending on the service, the information gathering can take twenty minutes up to an hour asking surface understanding into who you really are. Some people write a lot of detail and explain what they want and others write a sentence or two. Notice, I said the question-and-answer section will ask who you are, yet the person will basically wright the "Deal Breakers". This is my first indication of following directions. The Dating app or services, I use the terms interchangeably, can reveal hobbies, travel interests, cultural differences, retired or close to retirement and other basic information.

A personal picture or pictures are typically included in the profile and tell their own story. Pictures in my experience are of little or no help or value. This is where the book Blink, by Malcolm Gladwell comes to mind. The book in general states we all make decisions in a "blink of an eye." That was my takeaway of the book, although I am simplifying a deep subject. It can be said when any of us sees a picture of anything we create a judgement. This is especially true with personal pictures posted on dating sites. When we look into the camera on a cell phone, computer, or actual camera most people do not like what they see. Thus, we retake the pictures hoping for an improved vision or version of ourselves. I suggest finding a comfortable space in a park or backyard and have a friend or family member take a nice picture of you. The dating service picture will benefit and you will get more profile interest. Many people include older vacation photos with lots of scenery and very little personal detail. Pictures are taken on a family farm with pets and farm animals. Ladies, men are not interested in these pictures. I personally find interesting the pictures taken in full ski gear with ski goggles. I have also witnessed most senior web site pictures posted with parents, children, grandchildren, and other friends. Please, I beg you to keep family pictures out of the profile. This guidance is more for safety reasons. You don't know who is looking at your pictures. I understand woman are very proud of their living parents, children, and grandchildren, but a Dating site is not the place for these pictures. For me personally, it is a major turn off. Men traditionally are on these Dating sites for entertainment and to find a bed partner or a one-night stand. I mentioned this earlier in the book. I strongly suggest an updated picture of just you in a comfortable location. Keep the bathing suits and suggestive clothing in the closet. Keep the family photos and pictures of ex or passed husbands off the social medium.

Men, I didn't forget about you. Women don't understand the shirtless pictures. The pictures from a Go-Pro of you surfing or dragging out a deer with budging muscles, or water skiing. I don't suggest posting pictures posing in front of your monster truck, custom car, or with your Ex. If you like chew or smoke your oral hygiene with missing teeth or stained teeth is not appreciated. If you are on a dating app and want to impress a woman; especially in the senior years, think on their level. Post a picture with a sport jacket, comb your hair, remove the ball cap, and look grown up. Yes, I looked at some of the men to see who my "competition" is and to my surprise, the woman had valid points in the "Deal Breaker" section.

When I see a close up of a face on a dating app profile, I wonder what the rest of the person looks like. Yes, I ask myself if the person is average weight of heavy-set or perhaps very thin comes to mind. I prefer a little chunky, plump, or overweight. The takeaway to this section is that we are all judgmental and make decisions, some with minimal thought in a blink of an eye.

For fun and entertainment, I joined three dating services for six months after Linda passed away. I did my homework as suggested earlier to find the safest one. My question really was to find out if these services or apps have changed much since my young twenties. As I remember at the time, I paid for a three-month subscription to receive full benefits for one dating app and paid for one month subscription to receive minimal benefits for another. The third service was promoted as free and was limited with basic subscription benefits. What appears to me to be unimportant information is requested from customers in dating sites, but the end goal for the dating apps is a business model to have you a long- time subscribing member with high hopes, but no promises. I do recall that paying a full price, about $100 for six months was a waste money. The woman and men were doing the same, signing up on multiple apps hoping from one dating app to another in the hopes of finding the man or woman of their dreams. As with anything important, it is not a quantity game, it's a quality game.

I dated several women in my youth and was not looking for love, rather just to have fun. The same was true when I joined as a widower, thirty years later. I will share an example of a **coffee shop date**: The dating app used an algorithm with the information I provided and matched me with several woman they thought I would be a good match for. I was shown several woman profiles in a matter of minutes and chose one profile based on a moment of seeing a picture. I sent that person a friendly note with a dash of humor. She responded with interest. She said through several messages, she was educated, owned her home, worked in government, and liked sailing. One deal breaker, I insisted on a phone conversation. She refused, thinking her number would appear and I could be a stocker. I like hearing a voice to listen for accents, how people think and if they can carry on a conversation. I let this deal breaker slide. In retrospect, now moving forward I would insist on the phone call after a texting conversation. We texted for weeks and shared a lot of information. Our personalities appeared to match and agreed to meet for coffee. I let her choose the coffee shop and we agreed on a time. I arrived on time, after navigating city traffic and found a place to park. I was actually nervous with excitement. Weeks of texting and hopes the dating app profile might be legitimate. I texted her for a drink request to be polite and have it ready at an empty table. She arrived, walked through the door and as I reached out to give her a gentle hug, she put both arms up to block me. What are you doing, she asked? I don't know you! I don't hug strangers. I wish I had a picture of my face. I am a people person and a hugger. OK…I replied. Let's sit down and continue our texting conversation. As she and I talked, I felt a high anxiety on both sides. She made a comment and I laughed and commented back. She said, if you are going to interrupt me again, I'm just going to talk over you. Clearly, this was not working. I should have just gotten up and walked out, but I wanted to be a gentleman. After fifteen minutes, she said she needed to get back to work. I replied, this was clearly a mistake and walked out.

Lesson learned: chemistry is everything. A picture is only a visual. I did not follow my usual insisting on a phone call that I am sure would have revealed the conversation standoff. I continued to use the dating apps, but not taken so seriously.

How my parents met: The romance of my parents is a great love story. My father was attending USC in Los Angeles and dating a student. Apparently, they were not compatible according to the girlfriend, but she put up with him. My father was a nerd from a well-to-do family cultured in the arts and loved the symphony. My father invited his girlfriend to a LA Philharmonic concert, and she politely declined. But she offered to introduce my father to her girlfriend, who was in the Master's program at UCLA, in Los Angeles. "She likes your kind of music". My father was introduced to my future mother and asked her to the symphony and she gladly accepted. They may not have known it then, but they were a match. They grew in love over the next four years while playing tennis and snow skiing during off time. They were driving in Los Angeles and as they went through an intersection a drunk driver went through a red light and T-boned their car. They were severely injured and both were in a coma with multiple broken bones. The story continues, that my mother was on life support for three months and final arrangements were in the planning stages. This event apparently brought the two families close together and they pooled their finances for "the best medical coverage money could afford". In the end, both my parents recovered over time and my mother went on to have three children. As a side story, it was said my mother was in the Masters program at UCLA and my uncle who attended USC went to my mother's apartment and found and assembled her Masters thesis. He brought the thesis to the Dean of Social science and explained the car accident and the paper was accepted. The accident clearly solidified the families and my parents lived happily ever after for the next 55 years. We are who we are, after my mother passed my father being an introvert stayed to himself for the most part. He and my aunt (mother's sister) talked frequently on the phone. He tried to keep up with my aunt as my mother did talking to her sister frequently, both sisters made it out of Germany before the concentration camps were built. My dad did not find my aunt a replacement for my mother and my aunt three months later passed from cancer. It was now eight months after my mother passed and my father was diagnosed with kidney failure. The doctor told our family, it was treatable with dialysis and he could go on with a fairly normal life. My father was alone for the first time in 92 years, despite having his three sons at his side. He decided he wanted to join my mother and declined the treatment. She was attractive, smart, cultured. They complemented each other. He passed in peace three weeks later. You ask, why share this family story about your parents? It's a classic love story of a couple meeting in college and growing a life together till the end, but at what age do we determine it's the end for finding love. The local Portland Oregon news organization aired a story about a couple in their 70's perhaps older who met in the isle of a grocery store. The man made the approach and they married in the same grocery store isle they met in.

I met a friend when I was eighteen years old who had deep technical skills and appeared socially awkward. He did not find dating or social events comfortable to attend. A person who enjoyed outdoor activities, hiking and back woods cross country skiing. Later in life, he attended college sponsored hikes and noticed a girl about his age joining the group. He really wanted to introduce himself, but lost his courage being the shy type. He attended the scheduled hikes for months before seeing the girl once again. This time he introduced himself and smiles on both faces said it all. He was a technical wizard with interest in computers and astrology. He often attended Star gazing parties on mountain peaks in the dead of winter, enduring freezing temperatures just looking at Stars with an armature telescope. She endured the cold long nights with him. She was a teacher and they taught each other as love blossomed. They were married and had two daughters. They shared the love and culture of musicals and plays sponsored by local schools and professional performances. Unfortunately, as the children reached three and five years old an illness took her life. Fifteen years later, he is a wonderful single dad, never again breaking that social comfort zone.

I was aware of profiles that stated, '**love to travel**'. Where do they like to travel and on what budget? Profiles that say, love to hike. Are they talking a casual two-mile hike or a ten-mile hike? I don't want to send the wrong impression, both my daughters met nice guys on dating apps, but I needed to be more alert to what was a deal maker or deal breaker is for me. I found myself not interested in pictures of large families with pictures of parents, children, and grandchildren. I responded to profiles and asked where I would fit in with a large extended family seen in a picture. The response was kind; after my mother, children, and grandchildren. Perhaps, after my dogs. There was clearly no place for me, or did I just need a hug, kiss, and to hold hands. Someone to have a meaningful conversation with.

Today, and my most recent dating experiences, I don't care how or where I meet women, but clearly it makes an impact down the road regardless of time. Time is abstract, meaning we may know someone for three days or three years, but somewhere in the future of the initial meeting can determine how the relationship develops. Coffee shops are relatively quiet, relaxing, and a good spot to meet people to take the edge off the safety factor some people are concerned with. In the past, I have met women at local coffee shops and on the coast at State Park viewing scenic spots. The venue does make a difference. As I mentioned earlier, my parents met on a blind date and symphony music was the catalyst to their relationship. Again, to revisit an earlier theme of how couples meet, I mentioned a longtime friend met his wife on a hike. The list of how people meet is endless, and really just takes an open mind to the possibilities.

The person who initiates the first meeting invitation from a dating site for a face to face first meeting is also an influence and tell sign of personality. I'm not going to get into the Alpha or dominant male animal in a particular group science, where a man tending to assume a dominant or domineering role in social or professional situations. I will simplify this pattern by saying there are introverts and extroverts. I am an extrovert and don't mind inviting a woman out if I think there is interest on my end to find out more about her.

I have met women on dating sites who took the lead (Alpha) and asked me out on a casual date. I accepted with nothing to lose, actually feeling flattered. Being approached by the woman, I feel I can make more relaxed decisions. If the date does not feel comfortable; oh well, I really had nothing to lose. However, if I ask a woman out, I feel I really want this to work out and it puts more stress on me to meet expectations.

In my single years, I was looking on a dating web site and reached out to a woman who was attractive in the posted picture. I read she was a counselor suggesting to me she was intelligent, caring, and successful. We agreed to a phone conversation and after a few seconds on the phone I recognized a voice of a smoker. She admitted to being a social smoker, however I did not see social smoker on her profile page. After a brief conversation she revealed that she lives in a mobile home park, common In the Pacific Northwest along riverbanks and coastal communities. I never lived in anything but a wood stucco home and sometimes think less of people in trailer parks and I am not a fan of cigarettes. We agreed to meet in person having nothing to lose. We met in the afternoon at a coffee shop, her choice for safety concerns. As we greeted each other I reached out with arms wide open for a hug and she put her hand out for a handshake. Expecting a hug, this handshake was not a good start for me. I was not feeling the warm greeting I was hoping to find. We talked for half an hour and I started to wonder about time looking frequently at my watch. During our conversation, I mentioned my recent past being married to a Bi-Polar woman. I asked if she had challenges in life too? Yes, she said being a recovering alcoholic. Trying to keep a poker face I realize in my mind I had no further interest. Perhaps I am drawn to people in crisis? We parted with a half-hearted hug and now I understand the term, chemistry, or lack thereof. You can't fake the magmatism of chemistry and even when you try to be kind and open minded there is no shame is admitting this is not a match and politely remove yourself.

◆

Society norms

By society's norms; in the dating scene I mean, what we perceive should be a natural fit for two people excluding chemistry. We think if a man and woman meet at a church, they are both good people. If a man and woman meet at a bar, they must like alcohol or to hang out with friends for some excitement.

We exclude in this narrow vision of perceived compatibility or chemistry, the chemistry that exists with two people as what I call the "lock and key" theory. I'm sure there is a more technical term, but I am keeping this simple.

When a couple hug: oh my, the sincerity of a "I care hug". I clearly know a sincere hug when I feel it. I believe I mentioned my hugging experience at the Synagogue after Linda passed. I walked into the Synagogue and was met at the door by three women. There was no romantic intension, but three women gave me a welcome hug and I felt immediately the "I care hug" from the "how are you my friend" hug. How are you my friend hug, the lock and key just don't match perfectly. However, arms reaching around your body embarrassing you and a gentle whisper; how are you, we miss Linda. The lock and key just fit and the door opens to your mind. In a romantic situation it is clearly different, but sincerity is conveyed in non-thinking body language.

The kiss for the first time on the lips there is an immediate brain chemistry that is undeniable. I say when two people kiss because I don't consider two people a couple until there is a connection and understanding that the two people want to be considered as one unit, a couple. Enough deep thought. When the two people kiss and how they kiss is so individual. Yes, one person may immediately put their tongue in the other persons mouth, a French kiss. This may or may not be enjoyable or acceptable to the other. Or to the other persons surprise, both might like it very much. I remember meeting a woman for the first time and giving her a kiss on the cheek. She was flattered and said, "how sweet". A half hour later I tried this move again and kissed her on the lips and she said, "that is more like it". As the evening progressed, I wanted to take this relationship to the next level, and she looked at me and said, "let me show you how it's done". She gave me a deep French kiss, and I was not into this at all. It felt like a tongue vibrator in my mouth, versus a discern a slow soft tongue trust that was equally shared. Getting into PG-13 rated territory now. My point is we had different ideas of romance and I stopped the romance at that point. A kiss is not just a kiss. I mentioned earlier in the book, going on a date and after the hike we were in her car about to go for an ice cream. I reached over to give the woman a deep romantic kiss, tongue, and all. After my kiss she was in shock. She had not been kissed like that since college. She liked the kiss, but stated she was a grown woman, not in college anymore. Clearly, not ready for the next step in the relationship. No more grandma kisses for me moving forward.

And hug for the first time, it's like a lock and key combination coming together. When I kiss and hug a woman for the first time, I sense a fit or I don't. Nothing can prepare me for the positive or negative response. I might feel the chemistry and she may not. It can also work where she feels the kiss is just right and I may think…it was so-so. It should be no surprise when you hear, he holds the key to my heart or I found the right chemistry, it just works. I mentioned a grandma kiss earlier, as not natural in a couples' relationship. The kiss and hug is meant well and the love is transferred, but it is not the same as the chemistry transferred in a genuine hug and kiss when either a younger couple embrace or an older couple embrace.

Society has norms that balance prejudice and comfort. We are unintentionally, prejudice against what we don't relate to or understand. I attend a cigar lounge and listen to comments from men and woman about couples who come into the lounge. Faith, appearance, and education of individuals is often the subject of conversation in the context of a match or companionship. I also hear similar comments at religious gatherings or sports events about what brings a couple together and the chemistry that naturally occurs. Bottom line, there is no right or wrong to attraction and none of us has the right to judge others. If it feels right to you, then it is the best compatible match and partner.

Pets

Pets are tied emotionally to a person and family members and there is typically a story of how the pet came into the family. Family pets can be any animal including dogs, cats, or birds, you name it. On a farm or ranch it is typical to find pets ranging from dogs, cats, horses, and rabbits to the unusual. From my experience, family pets are difficult to predict and will be guarded to accept a new stranger being introduced since they often are innately trained to protect. When I started dating women, I experienced dogs that fiercely protected their owner. I was told, "Oh he is gentle as a "pussy cat." Large or small, the dog or dogs need to be introduced to a stranger or new partner with love and care. A growl from a dog is a sign of respect and caution. It takes time to learn the behavior and gain the dog's trust. Same for cats, as they can act out too. On a ranch, a horse needs the same attention and respect as other animals. When I see a pictures of a woman or men on a dating app next to a horse, I realize it is a lifestyle and comes with a price and takes a lot of time. The person usually has little time to travel or they rely on hired help. I also see pictures of other livestock in a ranch setting and realize the time and commitment. It is common to see these pictures in the Northwest or Midwest.

I call on medical offices selling medical services and recall a story of a nurse meeting a Pastor in church. The nurse attended services for several months and the Pastor took a liking to her despite their significant difference in age. After several dates, he invited her to his ranch and introduced her to the livestock. She immediately became attached to the dogs and horses. The Pastor simply said, you are welcome to stay as long as you want or visit anytime. She eventually moved in and they married shortly after. Clearly, the Pastor read her genuine love for the ranch life.

I met my current wife who had a small dog, Sadi Jones. Sadi Jones was a rescue from an abusive home where the dog owner could not care for the dog. Jen, my current wife, agreed to take care of Sadi Jones and offered a loving home. They agreed, and Sadi Jones could not have been happier from that day forward.

I had a small dog (Chihuahua mix) too that was a rescue from the Humane Society. I was with my past wife and looking for a service dog. Small and easy to care for. I wanted Linda, at the time, to have a friend to walk, feed, and pet. A welcome distraction. We noticed the sign on a cage, "Cocoa is a lap dog and does not bark much." In the years to follow, it was all true. Cocoa was easy to handle and affectionate.

I have a cat, Lucas; I adopted from my eldest daughter's girlfriend, living in an apartment that had a no pet policy. At my daughter's urging, I took in the cat and gave her girlfriend a room to rent. I mentioned her earlier in the book.

Over time, the dogs and cat appeared to get along. The cat was dominant in my house and clearly let Sadi Jones know it. The cat would hide from my dog and jump out as a surprise, my dog would bark and growl and the cat ran away. The cat did the same for Sadi Jones and took a claw swipe and hit Sadi Jones in the eye. This cost us $1500 dollars to save Sadi Jones eye. I paid for part of the Veterinarian bill feeling partially responsible, although I warned Jen that Sadi Jones liked to provoke the cat. This is animal play, but Jen had never owned a cat and was not familiar with cat behavior. In the years to follow the game persisted. When Sadi Jones got older, she went partially blind and could not defend herself. The cat swiped at Sadi Jones again, getting in the eye once again. This was the last cat and dog fight. It is a reminder that pets need to be a delicate match and introduced with care and caution. My example is common and new partners should be aware of family dynamics among pet introductions.

Food

How can I introduce how people meet or find compatibility and not mention food? We all eat and have a so called 'diet'. The word diet in this use is not intended to mean 'a diet to lose weight' as many people might think. Diet simplified, is what we eat and broken down into a science of caloric intake. My definition of diet certainly took the fun out of food, didn't it? There are cookbooks loaded with recipes that actually focus on just that, taking the fun out of food. The recipes found in these cookbooks were intended for the significantly overweight population or BBW (Big Beautiful Woman), but equally translate for BHM (Big Handsome Men) too, to encourage eating food for nutrition and not for enjoyment or fun. From an early age, new parents are taught to use eating games to encourage babies and children to try new foods. "Open your mouth…here comes the Choo-choo". Does that bring back memories? These food games actually backfired on me. My mother encouraged me to eat bananas and apple sauce at the doctor's request, because I was skinny and potassium was encouraged. Today, sixty years later I am still a very picky eater and a healthy skinny. Unfortunately, this pattern transitioned to my children because I did most of the cooking. Thus, my children eat few vegetables or fruits, but high on carbohydrates. Traditionally, we are taught to eat several meals a day or maybe snack often. Yes, we all snack on food that is good for us, carrots for example or ice cream. OK, maybe ice cream is not so good for us, but so delicious.

We all come from different cultures where food often defines who we are. I grew up in Studio City, CA in a relatively Jewish community where conservative Jewish traditions encouraged a Kosher diet. Not for our family, we often ate at local Deli restaurants in Studio City, Woodland Hills, and Agoura Hills. Of course, Canters Deli in Los Angeles was a favorite where I ate large pastries and thick Pastrami sandwiches. The bigger the sandwich and larger the cheesecake the better. My family was not the stereotype overweight Jewish family, in fact my parents and grandparents were relatively thin. My parents and grandparents would treat my family on holidays and special occasions to this wonderful food.

I was fortunate in High School to have a HS sweetheart whose family owned GerAls Jewish deli in Van Nuys, CA. I would go to the deli everyday with my girlfriend and get a free lunch. On occasion, I would go to the deli alone and order the same sandwich at no charge. One day, I went to the Deli without my girlfriend and no money in my pocket and ordered the same meal. To my surprise, my girlfriend's father said; pay-up on this meal, I understand you broke up with my daughter. "I told him; we had a little spat" turning bright red. He replied, apron is in the corner and dishes are ready to be washed.

Favorite foods are a conversation regardless of in-person, phone, or text, to discuss cultural food differences and share favorite foods, spices, and flavors. What foods and recipes we grew up with can determine if spicy foods are a favorite leaning toward Japanese or Thai or if fresh spinach and seafood pasta should be made together as a romantic home meal with a glass of wine. BBQ might be a favorite as you can fire up the BBQ for ribs, steak, or Tri Tip roast. My current wife learned Jewish holidays often included Matza Ball soup and potato pancakes as I grew up. Making this meal together was exciting and somewhat romantic as we molded the Matza Balls fresh in our hands together. Sometimes Fried Matza (egg goo and Matza mixed together in a frying pan) was on the menu for breakfast. She learned to make outstanding soup and has mastered Fried Matza, even though she doesn't eat eggs.

A Food festival can be an idea for a fun dating event and learning experience for both partners. This can be planned around Food Festivals with regards to special diets. Cousins from the past met at a Conservative Jewish Synagogue and went to a Kosher food festival for a date. I can't say, leftover Kosher pizza is a favorite. Newport Oregon, known as the Dungeons Crab capital, has a Seafood Festival with local cuisine that is also a safe choice for Diabetics in moderation. My wife likes crab cakes and shrimp cocktails as a treat, but not a fan of Oysters on the half-shell. We compromise by walking past the strawberry cake table and stopping at the coffee booth for sugar free flavored coffee.

Specialized diets are followed for a variety of reasons, focusing on health, culture, and religion. It is common courtesy for both partners to sit down at a dinner and discuss personal diets and favorite foods and wines. There are Kosher foods, keto plans, Vegan diets, and vegetarian recipes.

My wife was on a Keto diet when we met cooking Chicken and broccoli every night. It was a diet plan from a "Eat for nutrition, Not for fun" cookbook for losing weight. I was on a See Food plan; I ate what I saw. We compromised our meal planning for a Win -Win dining experience. For heart disease stability, a chicken breast can be BBQed with no skin, half a potato, and vegetables. For diabetics, like myself I focus on a sugar free high protein plan to gain weight.

Grocery shopping as a couple and eating out at restaurants. My current wife does the grocery shopping often alone, knowing what we eat is healthy. During the holidays; I like eggnog, thus, I drink light eggnog or dilute straight eggnog with milk. She also pays for the groceries; thus guys, if this is your arrangement and don't see what you like in the refrigerator, go to the grocery store, and buy the groceries yourself. In my case, my wife likes to cook healthy meals and knows all my preferences; I am grateful for the gifts in my life.

Eating out on vacations or just enjoying local cuisine restaurant. Couples should decide the foods that are important to them and go out dates once a week or a month and share different dishes. Mexican, Thai, and BBQ foods can be spicy and should be planed ahead. Plop plop, Fizz fizz… if you're reading this book, it should resound with you. Foods of the world are endless decisions and casual or fine dining should be talked about according to the monthly budget. Dinner at a fine dining steak house in Colorado or Wyoming could set you back $150.00 for a couple on the low end. A trip to a Manhattan Deli for an original Pastrami sandwich and real Boston cheesecake will set you back the same. Both highly recommended. Diets are for keeping health in mind for the long run, Life is short and worth exploring new foods and treating yourself in the short run. This type of eating should be reserved for a celebratory event. This is just an example and I will allow you to fill in the wants and needs of dining. This section of food and diets has been well covered in thousands of books and articles worldwide and the US is still leading the world in diabetes and obesity. We simply love food.

Finances

I will say from the start how we budget money or finances is reflective of our culture and how we were raised. Meeting a future partner living month to month on social security is significantly different than meeting a person retired comfortably on a company pension, social security, and dividends from the stock market. The following chapter or section reflects stories and examples of what to ask or look for when you meet a partner.

Thus, I begin. 'Boys and their toys' and 'Diamonds are a girl's best friend' leads me to believe both genders who enjoy life as they should. Sometimes indulging in wants not exactly needs, as they prepare for retirement is a sign of maturity. Do we really need or use what we have? Finances covers a broad range of topics, a simple exchange of what both partners bring to a relationship. This would include spending and investing habits as well as retirement preparation. In fairness when I meet a woman, I am judging her, as I think she is evaluating me. What brand of purse she is carrying (Coach), shoes she is wearing (stiletto heels or tennis shoes), and jewelry she is wearing (diamonds to watch)?

If the woman is evaluating a man, me for example: a coach man bag, worn no name leather shoes, and jewelry (a ring of diamonds from my parents and a $10.00 1970's Casio watch). The watch is a huge woman turn off. I leave my Carita watch for nice occasions. My point is we all get the wrong idea about financial expression.

If I visit a woman's home, I am aware of outside yard care toys: boats in the yard ready to go water skiing or in disrepair? A recreational vehicle in the driveway ready for a road adventure or in disrepair. Inside the house, I am aware of visible art and furniture. As a woman approaches a house of a man, she is aware of yard care, boats, and RV's. As she enters the house, she is looking for signs of sports or hobbies. In my case, the woman would find a cared for yard and no toys. Inside she would find several cigar humidors and selected art with sentimental value. We all judge each other instead of a pleasant conversation asking about sport, hobbies, and how each other has prepared or is preparing for retirement. In other words, how do we handle money. I found my new wife and I share very similar spending and investment practices. This was comforting. We can go to an Art festival and admire the art and only invest in a painting if we agree.

I am financially stable earned over my lifetime. The women I have met and dated over time were across the board, having little to offer in a relationship to having financial security and still had education debt. This new connection can be tricky because we are meeting in our senior years and should be settling into our retirement with toys and education paid off. Family dynamics can get involved with children and grandchildren asking, what does the new partner bring into the relationship?

What we should ask ourselves, is did our new partner grow up struggling, comfortable, or privileged? The culture we grew up in can influence spending habits and what toys (boats, vehicles, RV's) they have and if they are owned, financed, and the condition they are in. We need to find that balance.

Example: I have a long-time friend a successful professional, middle aged, and divorced. He met a beautiful woman though a hobby they both love. Through business success he bought a house, found a repossessed Porsha, and an Aprilia motorcycle in a distress sale. He is a pilot and owns an airplane. He is smart and introverted and reads people well. He rewarded himself with the woman of his dreams when he found his new future wife singing in a chore. Together they create their own harmony and shared the love of music. To see them together is a privilege.

Example: A woman friend from High School (HS girlfriend) had a complicated life yet seemed to juggle it all well. She had a successful business with her ex-husband and is leaning toward retirement. In her fifties, she attended a party where she met a new partner with less to offer in the relationship. She explained, "He is nice to me and makes me happy. He deserves what I have to offer." The man found a woman who is successful and offered an easy lifestyle toward early retirement. She was adopted and came from a family with mental illness and has occasional bouts of mania. She is not afraid to spend money to enjoy life.

Example: Another woman friend is a widow and retired from a government job. She inherited a beautiful home, vehicles, and is living comfortably. She has three children, one with a substance abuse problem in and out of treatment. She is smart, not needy, and whoever she brings into her life will bring equal financial resources to the relationship.

Example: A longtime friend lost her husband in his fifties to alcohol poisoning. They were a good match; he was a published writer and she a successful territory manager . In a chance of fate, I lost Linda a year after my friend lost her husband. Unfortunately, the loss of our spouses ties us together more than our connection in the medical field. . Forward eight years and despite both of us being very selective in the partners we were dating, I remarried. She is smart, has a great job, and is a successful businesswoman . She uses online dating as a main source to meet single men because she lives in an outlying community. She is willing to travel hours for a date, but admittedly, most of the guys she has met are not what they appear to be online. She shared with me, both she and a man traveled hours to spend the day together. Both had a good time that day and he asked if they should go to his room for the night, referring to a hook-up. She said she would see him in the morning and at age fifty she is not in college anymore. She was tired and ready for sleep. "Guys, know your audience". Not every date is going end in a hook-up. She texted the man in the morning, she was ready to meet for breakfast. He said he was already halfway home, packed up at 5:00 am and called her inappropriate names. Remember I mentioned maturity and communications and discussing tough subjects out. The man was expecting more than what was promised. She says men are jerks....and more. She has high standards (or does she?) with a good job and strong financial portfolio.

Through these examples, I wanted to bring to your attention there is no perfect relationship as we meet in our senior years. We need to learn how important is it to have a conversation about finances, family struggles, and what to expect in the future.

Credit /debit cards or outstanding loans: Does the person you are meeting have one or several credit cards? Are they paid for in full every month or are they on a payment plan? Do they use a debit card or cash? These are questions I ask myself and observe as we go through a day of fun. When it is time to pay for an event or meal, do they pull out the wallet or purse with no hesitation. I can always ask directly and observe the response if they find the question rude. I do the slow draw and watch their response. My experience is Jennifer, is a fast draw and pays with cash or a with debit card. I pay with cash or with credit card.

Do you see an RV in the driveway rarely used in need of repair and expired tags or a RV in the driveway rarely used with updated tags? Is there a fully equipped ski boat in the driveway, with expired tags? Walking into the house or apartment for the first time what did I see? Art or wall pictures that reflected my taste or not my style? These are examples of what I experienced as I dated woman and tried to understand their values. Reading this, the audience could say, its none of your business and just walk away if you don't like what you see? My thinking reflects spending and investing patterns. I frequently hear from past friends who connected with the wrong partner. I had no idea they spent money like that? I don't want to bring up pain points again, but mania associated with mental illness presents often with uncontrolled and unexplained spending with both men and woman. In mania men can spend impulsively on fine cigars, gun collections, and golf supplies. Woman in a mania phase might spend impulsively on art, clothes, shoes, and accessories. Mania can also manifest in excessive gambling and drinking habits.

Good Healthcare Practices

In our senior years, good healthcare is a broad subject covering many topics that can't be ignored. This is especially true as individuals in their 50's, 60's and beyond meet future partners. There are taboo subjects and misinformation 'rumors circulating' about what are good health practices. These life decisions can affect financial decisions too. I will merge prior sections of the book at this time to prove a point, everything about human healthcare is inter-related. For example, I have been advised by my doctor to eat properly and exercise on a regular basis since I have been diagnosed with type-two diabetes. My lifestyle changes include relieving stress through swimming to eating a low carb diabetic diet. Everyone has a health history and depending on how active we were growing up and in raising our family also determines future healthcare needs. Health insurance and medical coverage will have an impact on future budgets and retirement expenses. I am rounding the corner on signing up for Medicare, not an option I can run away from. My wife has PERS (retirement plan from Oregon State) and she will have a retirement plan with a major insurance carrier. None of these options will save us from high medical bills if a catastrophic medical emergency arises. When I mention major medical complications, I am referring to cardiac disease, diabetes, stroke among other medical issues.

In my profession as an account manager in the healthcare industry, I am fortunate to call on specialty medical groups and witness firsthand the patients in their 50's and beyond "seeing the doctor" for the unexpected visit. For example, in the Renal (Urology) specialty I see men with collection bags at their side as they slowly walk in and out of the Urology clinic. Enlarged prostate is common in men and hyperactive bladder is common among men and woman and has an immediate life altering impact. For men, intimacy is directly impacted, sleep disruption is common, and limited outdoor activities. All of which should be sympathized with by a new partner at this stage of life. My point is both sexes have physical and mental struggles to overcome. It is difficult to understand until you are personally delt these cards in life.

Other age- related health complications are related to orthopedics (bad knees and back), cardiology (heart problems), and gastroenterology (colitis). There is no end to health- related life impact conditions but bringing an empathetic mindset into a new relationship is a gift in itself.

During my career I have sold diagnostic lab tests and I discovered the Naturopathic, ND community. Doctors who test for the balance in your body chemistry and focus on preventative medicine. This specialty provider can uncover hidden diseases evolving before the symptoms complicate life. The patients I have met in Naturopathic offices and had conversations with are happy with their treatment.

It is played out time and time again, how seniors come together with good intentions and healthcare catches them off guard. How do you plan ahead? For starters, I would suggest having multiple conversations over time regarding medications you are taking. The couple should make a list of the medications, dose, and time of day the medications are taken. Put that list on a kitchen tack board or in a purse or wallet. This information can be taken to a routine medical appointment or used in an ER setting. For example, I went to the ER the other week at 3:30 AM for severe abdominal pain. The triage nurse asked if I was on any medication and I threw a zip lock bag with medications at her. She needed to enter the medications and dose into her computer to generate my ER chart. I was not following my own advice. I worked in the ER as an EMT, I should know better! This simple act of listing my medications would have made the RN's job so much easier and the ER team could have brought me back to a treatment room faster. The continuous conversations will include blood type, surgeries over the past fifteen years, and just overall health related issues.

So, I ask; who is diabetic, overweight and has high blood pressure? Unfortunately, millions of Americans. That was similar to my situation with diabetes and a stagnant exercise program. With my doctor as a guide, I agreed to reexamine my diet and to start swimming weekly. These simple changes significantly helped me rebalance my life.

In fairness, my doctor could have suggested sharing a romantic healthy meal once a week with my wife. These small steps can lead to the use of scented oils and a shared massage to relieve stress and with approval from your partner followed by close intimacy. But doctors are no fun, and this advice would actually be followed when we find the right partner. So yes, bringing a new partner into your life and re-introduce the emotional connections that is actually healthy and reduces stress. Each person can apply the cologne and perfume you chose for each other as suggested earlier. Inhale the fragrance as the body chemistry works with each person. Embrace with **hugs** that bring us together human to human. Slowly and with permission, remove the barriers of clothes if you feel it's time and learn to expose the essence of who we are and build trust. Embrace what you see and appreciate what you have before you. No judging a beer belly or a woman for the children she birthed. Gentle **kisses**, again slowly exploring the gift you have. **Holding hands** is so comforting even applying a warm scented lotion as each person caresses the hand they hold. This is when **conversation** is so important. Gently talk or whisper what you want from your partner. These actions once a week or once a month might actually help you eliminate a hypertension pill from your life, increase circulation, and leave both partners with smiles of gratitude.

I woke up this morning at 7:00 as a usual with the help of my alarm clock and the smell of my wife's perfume was still lingering in the air. I could also smell my men's chalone oil on my pillowcase. My cat was lying beside my pillow purring loudly and licking my fingers, a reminder it is time for breakfast. I got out of bed my body slightly sore from the prior evening's activities. A good sore, so grateful for my wife's affection.

I got in the shower and I did a self- prostate examination remembering a good friend of mine found prostate cancer twice in this same fashion. Woman can perform a self -breast examination in the shower too. I walked over to my closet and looked for a nice casual suit to wear, always dressing for success in sales not knowing when opportunity may knock. The same thought should go through our mind as a widow or widower, always going out looking and feeling our best.

My wife walked into the bedroom with a cup of coffee for me and kissed me good morning. She complemented me on my suit and said, 'looking good'. I told her I am dressing for success and trying to keep up a work ethic and self- image. In our senior years, confidence and support is so important to maintain a healthy lifestyle. This last paragraph is a great example of how important **conversation** is in moral support and confidence building.

I walked into the kitchen for a fresh cup of coffee and started cooking my breakfast. In my opinion breakfast is an important meal to start my day and allows for a snack before a 12:30 to 1:00 lunch, especially for a diabetic. I catch up on my emails looking for a positive reply from prior submitted job applications. I won't bore you with my routine, but I am making a point. We all wake up in the morning with inherited stresses or concerns of the daily life. We can choose to be concerned and take action on those subjects we have control over or let life issues control us. We choose the partner we wake up with. A partner we can bounce ideas off of and it is always a 60/40 relationship both ways. Meaning we give and take equally in a relationship. Give your partner a gentle hug of support or words of encouragement. Have a morning routine in place that is easy to follow and allows for flexibility. This is a healthy relationship.

I met a neighbor at my coast house who is retired and single. He walks the paths in the community several times a day and we share the same brief comments when we cross paths. I am walking the paths with my 35mm camera looking for pictures for my book. I hope you approve of my selections. Thus; when I cross paths with my neighbor, I see a man who would benefit from a partner to share life and conversations with. Some people would reply to my thoughts…your neighbor is just fine enjoying retirement. He is happy and satisfied in life and does not need your help or constant need for conversation that you search for. These opinions are valid; however, if he found a partner to share life with, I think you would see a happier person and in general a healthier person.

Another part of a healthier life is taking our medications as prescribed. No, I'm not reaching out of bounds on medications. I take three medications a day for high Cholesterol, high blood pressure, and glucose control. We eat out often and I don't usually have my medications with me. When we return home, my wife will remind me to take my medications. I could take the pills in the morning, but my pharmacist suggested the glucose medication to help control my diabetes is more effective taken before dinner. My wife is taking several medications and uses a pill box to sort and manage her daily medications, what a great idea. Senior age people are on medications for a multitude of health-related issues and sometimes the same medication multiple times a day, do what is needed to simplify the routine.

We are often forgetful as we age, medications to stabilize mental illness is also taken several times a day and is easily forgotten. It is smart for both partners to be familiar with the medications each person is taking, the dosage, and pharmacy used to fill the medications. I know mail order programs are popular with seniors to save money, yet am not a fan of mail order. If a couple goes on a vacation and forgets one or all the medications, I like the option of calling our neighborhood pharmacy and requesting an emergency supply called into a local pharmacy. The pharmacist can call the doctor and request an emergency dose or call the local pharmacy directly. Warning, this will not be the case for pain medication. This has happened to me twice in my life and having a personal relationship with a local neighborhood pharmacy is helpful. Be aware of your neighborhood pharmacy hours of operation and it is a good idea to get to know the pharmacist on a personal name basis too. Some chain pharmacies that I will not mention by name are closed on weekends.

Some medications are given by infusion (IV) and injection called Biologics. Outside of a hospital setting these medications may require a prior authorization from your insurance, an infusion service in limited supply, and are expensive with limited or no insurance coverage. These medications will not be available in a local pharmacy. I mention this rare and odd entry into the book because these biologic medications are a significant cost to a tight retirement budget.

For a new partnership (couple) who loves to travel, I suggest the couple writing down their medication list including dose, and time to take the medications. Place this paper in a zipper lock bag and place in a safe (memorable) location within the luggage with easy access. Pre-planning for an unforeseen medical emergency, the list is easily accessed for paramedics, or an emergency room visit. I worked in the emergency room as an emergency medical technician and recognize the value of this information and planning ahead of time to prevent stress in a stressful situation.

Another suggestion is writing this medical information on a computer and saving it to a flash drive. It is small and can be kept in a wallet, back-pack or purse for easy access. I also suggest a week or more prior to leaving on your vacation to call your doctor office and ask for a copy of your current and relevant medical records, especially with a complex medical history. At the senior age, we all have a relatively lengthy medical chart. This was done and helpful when I was in Hawaii and took Linda (first wife) to an Urgent Care for a broken finger in a fall.

Who has a history of **mental illness**? Unfortunately, more people than you might think. In my life circle of friends and family: my prior wife Linda, my Grandfather, and a close friend's wife. Mental illness is not one disease, not a light subject, or easily admitted to a stranger. There can be several medications used on a daily basis and ongoing counseling sessions to manage the dosing of these medications. Mental illness is a lifestyle and clearly falls into good healthcare practices. Medication monitoring is critical and can be time sensitive in national travel time changes and international travel. Medications for mental illness management can be costly because most insurance companies don't cover new brand name medications and often insist on covering a cheaper generic medication first. Mental illness does not know a generic medication from a name brand. Thus, frequent therapy sessions are often required for medication adjustments at additional costs. When you first meet a new partner and medical history is discussed, honesty and transparency are important. Ask if mental illness is part of their life personally or in the family. Family members with mental illness can be mentally draining and add additional stresses to a person's lifestyle. If you meet a new partner and they admit to multiple relationships or several divorces, mental illness could be a reason why. For people reading this in a mental illness support system NAMI (National Alliance for Mental Illness) or other support groups, I am bringing awareness to a subject that should be talked through, especially with a new relationship in the development stages. I am not advocating running away from this relationship, although I admit in the beginning stages of the book I suggest avoiding relationships where mental illness is a known factor This is from my experience after thirty years. Admittedly, if a person in our senior years has a diagnosed mental illness and is well managed I believe you should follow your heart. Everyone can lead a healthy lifestyle with mental illness being well managed and do well with a new partner as long as there is compassion.

This is a tough and emotional subject to talk about publicly and with transparency and discussed in the open. I am able and willing to lead that discussion in any public setting. I have attended public talks led by MD's and PhD's in their CV at support groups, I thank them for participating in the conversation. They are well trained in the disease state, but in fairness they did not live the lifestyle.

First date, Second date

Bringing the sections together I challenged myself to have fun and think of the seasonal activities and what a first date could be for a new partnership to learn about each other. I challenge you to share your own thoughts and ideas and pictures.

Winter activity dates:

- **Museums:** In Portland Oregon we are proud of our OMSI Natural History Museum. Portlanders are also fond of the Oittock Mansion, a historic residents turned into a museum.
- **Snow skiing:** The drive to the resort and sharing an adventure of the fresh mountain snow and sitting beside a lodge fire having cider. Introducing stories and fond life memories.
- **Storm watching on the coast as waves crash along the shore.** Stopping at a pub for a beer or seafood meal.

- Crabbing along a coastal community in the Pacific Northwest. Usually found at a coastal harbor as you discuss what boat you want to buy. Crabs caught can be cooked at local restaurants in Newport Oregon or Tillamook Bay.

- **Winter photography:** Grab your phone or 35mm camera as I did for this book and take your first pictures of fond memories.

- **Kite flying:** This is a fun activity that often brings back childhood memories to share. An activity done in a fun open space with great physical activity that you don't really think about. Lincoln City, Oregon sponsors an annual Kite flying event with people participating from all over the world. It is worth doing research to find out if your community sponsors a similar event. Remember to bring a jacket and prepare for windy conditions. I guarantee laughs and smiles.

- **Glass blowing:** a growing hobby in the Pacific Northwest with offered classes: Google for the nearest glass blowing workshop if you like hands on art entertainment. Watch in awe or take home a memory after a class. Found in Lincoln City, Oregon.

- **Antique shopping and book store hunting.** This activity is really all year round.

- **Vintage store shopping:** Where I have found vintage Levi clothing. It is fun modeling for each other and sharing stories of the past while looking for treasures.

- **Cooking lesion:** learn to cook a meal for each other.

- **Pottery class.** Make a new piece of art to share.

Spring dates:

- Photography of the new blooms and repeat Winter fun.
- Take a jet boat ride in Portland Oregon or Grants Pass. Thake a whale watching boat tour in Newport or Depoe Bay Oregon.
- Bird watching in Spring and Fall is migration season. Great photography opportunities.
- Time for fishing in the ocean or lake.
- Row Boats and kayaks are for rent on the coast or inner lakes. Time to get some great exercise.
- Warm up your tennis or pickle ball arms. Another great activity for exercise.
- Agat hunting along the shores of rivers and coastal communities.
- Golf
- Garage sale hunting: Find recycled treasures.

Summer dating activities:

- Kite flying: Time to run again
- Sky diving in the Pacific Northwest is a true head rush, once in a lifetime.
- Sailing, Water skiing, row boat, kayak, holding hands walking along the coastal shores, Tennis time again,
- Try surf or wind surfing lessons: laughs and smiles to follow.
- Summer photography: never a dull moment.
- Drive in the mountains or coast.

- Take advantage of Summer food festivals and concerts
- Golf
- Garage sale hunting continues.
- Antique malls and book stores follow a theme

Fall dating activities:

- Leaves are changing and a romantic drive through mountain passes or coastal routes is always mood lifting, convertible hood down if at all possible.
- Fall photography brings out the colors in trees, streams, and lakes. Mountain hikes and combining photography has no boundaries. Laughs, smiles, and selfies encouraged.
- Bird watching is fun in estuaries. Fall migration can fill the sky with unparalleled beauty.

Meeting my current wife, Jen

I went to a local bar a year after Linda passed away just to see what so many people in the local cigar lounge talked about with such passion. Conversations about "hot looking woman", music, and a great place to chill. I was never really a big drinker or comfortable walking up to a woman just to say hello. My go-to drinks are red wine or Rum Chata on the rocks. People reading this will say "What kind of drinks are those? Get real…" Like I said, I never really developed a taste for drinks I gained a real liking for. Friends at the cigar lounge would recommend a great Scotch with a fine cigar. One time I ordered a Scotch and went out on the patio to light up a cigar to pair with the Scotch. Oh my, , yuck! The Scotch was terrible. Later at the cigar lounge; I shared my experience, and was laughed at. I was told, you need to build up a taste for fine Scotch. Whatever, I will stay with my red wine and Rum Chata.

Over a short period of time going to this local bar, I developed a friendship with a woman. No chemistry at all after a brief hug and friendship kiss. She was in her mid-forties, blond hair, a little overweight, and smart. Nice to have a conversation with, she knew I was single and looking. She brought to my attention the bar tender. She said "she is younger, mid-forties, long curly brown hair with only a speckle of gray. She has a warm grin and bright smile that most people like about her'. The woman I was with said, walk up to the bar and order a drink? Out of a man's thinking I mentioned, she is a bit overweight? The woman replied, back to me, and you are older, and thinning...despite your best intensions. Your no prize either. When you order your drink, don't forget to give her a big tip! I walked up to the bar and ordered a simple drink and saw her facial expression and smile that other people admired. She wore an appropriate lower cut top and I asked if that was intentional? Probably, she replied... a nice smile for a well- deserved tip maybe? I saw a bartender who enjoyed her job, worked well with the customers, and made the best of a working situation. I took out my wallet to pay and wrapped a twenty-dollar bill around my business card. I told her to "call me if you're - not a tease? She repeated, if I'm not a tease"? I replied I don't like playing games, too old for that. I expected nothing in return. Several days later I got a text asking if I wanted to meet for coffee? We met at a local coffee house and as we approached each other, our arms opened wide to give and receive a warm and sincere hug and kiss hello. No Grandma hug or Grandma kiss. Just a warm and inviting sincere embracing hug. After a comfortable two -hour conversation, we said goodbye in the parking lot. Again; a very warm and sincere kiss and hug. This date was a good example of why I miss, hugs, kisses, and conversation. I invited her out for dinner and she accepted.

A week later we met at her house for a dinner date. Her house is in a nice neighborhood with a simple yet functional landscaped front yard groomed by a gardening company. I rang the bell and she answered moments later. She was wearing a comfortable outfit, long hair tied back with a barrette, and no make-up that I noticed. She greeted me with that warm smile, gentle kiss, and sincere hug. This was clearly her ongoing theme of greeting people, genuine, loving, and sincere.

As I entered the living room it was furnished with a balance arrangement of well- maintained furniture in a conversational pattern. No stains or rips seen in the carpet, and furniture covers to protect from her dog. I noticed paintings on the wall and some paintings leaning against the walls on the floor later to learn she liked to paint in her spare time but didn't think her work was very good. She asked me if I wanted her to put on paint (make-up)? No need I replied.

We drove to a local Italian restaurant; the mostly full parking lot reflected a popular eatery. I got out of the car and reached out to hold her hand as we walked to the restaurant entrance. I felt her hand grasp mine. We chose a local middle of the line Italian restaurant and enjoyed great conversation. During meal courses I held her hand. This is clearly a non-verbal gesture that is as important, if not more important than hugs, kisses, and conversation. Hand holding needs no explanation, is harmless, and says I care in body language and sets off a brain chemistry to say I care.

I remember my parents had a code while holding hands. My father would squeeze my mother's hand four times…Do You Love Me? My mother would squeeze his hand three times… Yes, I Do. My Dad would squeeze again twice… How Much? And both would clutch hands hard. I witnessed this ritual in party settings and public places. I kept the tradition with Linda, and now my current wife.

We continued our dinner conversation, the check arrived and she grabbed it saying "this is on me". I don't like owing anyone anything. From that day forward, we take turns paying for meals out.

Intimacy and Closeness

Keeping this PG-13

At this stage of our life as I have written, we are in our forties and beyond and it really does not matter because chances are you found a partner to be close to. If it was through a dating service app, some barriers may have been naturally removed and being intimate is a little easier. But significant cultural and religious differences may present a stigma about new relationships we all need to understand. In code, this means; cool your jets and read your audience. In relationships try to relate to your partners wants and what they perceive as physical needs.

This is how I approached my new circumstance. First, we had a heart-to-heart talk and agreed to move the relationship to the next level. This reminds me of a huge mistake I made months before I met my new bride. I was on a dating service app and connected with a woman I though was a good match. We agreed to meet in Eugene,

Oregon and she suggested a hike. She was a probation officer and in very good physical shape. We met at a local park, and greeted each other with a hug and I kissed her on the cheek. She didn't seem to mind. We went on an eight-mile round trip hike, during which we held hands and had a great conversation. We agreed to grab a bite to eat and she wanted to drive us in her car to a restaurant. Sitting in the car, I asked if I could kiss her? With a big smile, she said yes that would be OK. I gave her a big kiss and yes, full French kiss tongue and all. I really don't know what came over me. She pulled back and said, WOW, I have not been kissed like that since high school. I asked if she liked it? She replied, 'we are adults now, parents, grandparents...we are not in high school. Your moving way to fast'. She politely asked me to get out. I'm not that kind of woman. OK, I learned my lesson, read my audience and ask first.

After our talk and drawing boundaries, we could agree on, we decided to go shopping for cologne and perfume, actually fun. We went to a fragrance shop in a local mall and had fun smelling colognes for me and perfume for her. For men; you dip a stick into a bottle and let it dry a moment, then with the stick at three or four inches away take a slight sniff. We shopped for a couple hours and bought a bottle for her and I. Funny, about this experience... we attended a Saturday Market in our community and walked by a men's shaving booth. He was selling essential facial oils and beard soaps. My girlfriend now sniffed the soap and oil. "Mmmm, smell this honey." It was so smooth on my face and complemented the shaving soap. That weekend we went out for dinner and she wore her new perfume and I put on my shaving oil following a close shave. Now before you let your imagination run wild, we were complimenting each-others gifts and how we appreciated the gesture. Ladies and gentleman, you can also have the same provocative fun choosing clothes. We went to the same shopping mall and she bought me skin tight Levies. That is what she wants me to be seen in. I bought her a tank top and denim jeans too.

Take each other out and treat for a pedicure and manicure. We did and I felt great after using my birthday certificate. Age does not dictate holding hands walking in the mall while sharing an ice cream cone together with a gentle kiss between bites. Discovering fragrances to match chemistry while kissing his neck or treating for a professional massage. Give each other a gentle neck rub with your partners permission.

I am reminded of a time I briefly dated a massage therapist I met her on a dating service app. She worked at a lodge in the resort town of Hood River Oregon. She invited me to have a couple's massage at the lodge from her colleagues. Again don't let your mind wonder, It was professional and therapeutic and I understood her gift as a profession. She even taught me several relaxing techniques I use to this day. We were left in private for a few minutes after the message session with our towels in place, to simply enjoy the moment. I guess we instinctively understood our boundaries and were ahead of our time and comfort zones.

There is a peaceful and loving nature in a couple's exploration and sharing a bathing experience in a bath or shower. Again; we are adults, likely with children and grandchildren and we seek the approval first from our partners. My girlfriend is thirteen years my junior and out of boredom suggested we visit an adult shop. This is a good way to explore comfort zones, pleasure, and ideas of what worked before and what was a waste of money used infrequently in the past. There is always advice to seek from the employees who should have knowledge of the products, if not personal experience to advise. No, I'm not going to get into the details, but will say prices can get high if you are not careful. We chose some fragrance oils and lotions to use during bathing. Oils can add a nice sent to a bath and lotions can be applied gently to a partner after a shower. We could have walked out with two hundred dollars or more of products if we listened to the salesgirl. Instead, we invested forty dollars and the essential oils still stand unopened in our bath area.

◆

That's What Friends are For

This reminds me of the Elton John song with Deon Warwick: That's What Friends are For. A song explaining the value of true friendship. I believe I had the song played at my first wedding reminding me that I was marrying my best friend. I mention this because learning from the friends your new partner introduces you to could be a glimpse into your partners personality and this also played out with my new wife.

I was introduced to a fantastic couple in their early forties who dog sat for my then girlfriend. I realized how much animals, especially saving dogs meant to Jen as our relationship developed. We attended Humane Society fundraisers and I was surprised on the donation amounts during open fundraising auctions. So, it did not come as a big surprise to learn, Jen was paying hundreds of dollars a month in dog sitting fees while working a full-time job. In time, I would learn more about Jen's personality through this couple than I could on my own. The man was an environmental chemist and worked in agriculture. He was involved with the Cannabinoid industry and understood the brain chemistry and addiction process. The woman was a true artist, and shared that passion with Jen. Over time, Jen would share pictures and paintings she had done. Jen is very selective on the friends she invited into her life. At one time, she allowed this couple to stay in her house for several months as she was moving into my home. They needed a transition place to stay and Jen needed to think about consolidating her personal positions. The hand-me-down living room couch, love seat, and chair that was originally donated to Jen by this couple two years ago, needed to fit in my house. Jen found the living room set comfortable and clearly expensive when the set was new. The woman used her artist and interior design creativity and worked out a comfortable place in my home. This couple taught me the kind of people Jen brings into her life with love and embracing nature she has.

On my side, there is a life-long friend I met at the age if sixteen. He became a career Coast Guard member and retired as a Lieutenant Commander. He met a woman at the Red Cross and over time they became friends and married. She became a nurse. They met Jen during a visit to Los Angeles and immediately clicked as Jen recognized the same sarcastic humor in my life-long friend as I did. It is amazing how much we can learn from friends of people we meet. Clubs we associate through and hobbies we share. Jen has friends who are my age and all very well educated. I have friends similar in age and education. Thus, if we had a party with our friends of a lifetime, it would be a well-balanced event.

Moving In Together

The decision to combine households was easy for me. After all, I was not the one moving my possessions out of my house I had been living in for twenty years. Thus, I suggest the partner (me) who has the home or apartment being moved into to have understanding and compassion for the other partner (Jen) giving up or making the larger sacrifice or commitment. My girlfriend (Jen) at the time moving into my home asked that privacy be a number one priority and my daughters can't just walk into the house "Willy-Nilly" as they have done in the past. 'This is no longer their childhood home; this is now our home." What I did not expect was a conversation explaining to my children, that they needed to call first before coming over. Knock on the door or ring the doorbell and wait for us to let you in the house. Like any other visitor, you can't just walk in the house anymore because you don't live here anymore. This was a new mindset for me too; I needed to understand my roommate, girlfriend, and I were living separate lives under one roof. My roommate at the time (a guy mid-twenties) told me he woke up at ten in the morning after working a late shift and walked into the kitchen to find my eldest daughter sitting there reading her mail. He could have walked into the kitchen "butt naked". Not a good situation, but funny looking back. He did mention this to me, and I did just pass it off as an unfortunate circumstance. No longer, my girlfriend needed to trust me and the house rules needed to be enforced to earn trust.

Moving in together is a huge step in a relationship and demonstrates commitment to each other. I admit it was a fairly easy transition for me, yet a huge struggle and considerable sacrifice from my girlfriend. Something important to consider during this moving process is everyone has a past history often reflected in house hold items, such as furniture, silverware or family China passed down from generations or with a strong emotional connection that we will take with us. In my case; the couch in my house is older and a moss green that I don't like, but my father took daily naps on. I have a strong emotional tie to it. The queen bed in my guest room is the same bed my parents slept in and my father passed away on and yes, I feel a strong connection. Yes, I can hear an audible Oooo, yuck, but it is after all just a bed. I don't tell guests, by the way, my dad passed away in that bed. But laying on that bed, again I feel close to my parents. I also have the original dressers my parents were given by my grandparents as a wedding gift. They are real wood and in great condition after 80 years. I was asked by my brothers to take these items as we cleaned out my parent's apartment for the last time and was lucky to have a moving van parked outside. The emotional connection has only grown stronger over the years. My girlfriend at the time has items she is tied to also. She brought with her an old desk, dresser, and living room couch set. We are fortunate to have the space in my house. The hodgepodge of things may look like a collection of old and somewhat new to those who enter our home, but to us, it is who we are. Never felt more at home and at peace. I would never ask my new partner to get rid of anything that had strong memories, nor her to my things.

Our circumstances helped in this transition. She has friends who are retired and moved to Mexico. They need to return to the United States every six months to maintain their Visa's. At her suggestion, she decided to offer her home to her friends for an extended three months as she prepared to move into my home. Timing could not have been better. Most of her furniture and kitchen items stayed in her home, for her house guests to use as we moved pictures and clothes during the initial moving phase. Moving her items from a smaller home with two bedrooms and one bath and 1000 square feet to my home of four bedrooms and three bathrooms and 2200 square feet made this transition far easier. We wanted to create our own personal space and we joined our lives together. To add another dimension into this already complex transition; I had a roommate who moved in two years prior, but we were all good friends by now. I understand people would suggest the roommate leave, but he was a young man who had advanced technology "computer skills" to help me out in my technology challenged world. He was an excellent cook and helped clean around the house. Thus; for extra rental income, a great cook, house cleaning benefits…why rock the boat? For months we all worked well together and as the time grew shorter for the friends to stay in her home, my girlfriend wanted to know about our future plans? The time came for her friends to return to Mexico. She did not want to leave my house if marriage plans were on the horizon. She discovered through conversation with her cousin, they were looking to re-locate. She offered her house again, but this time for the long term. We decided it was time to empty her remaining furniture and household items into my house. I am simplifying this process. It is a highly emotional blending of households. It can also be a stressful time to blend households, yet also a time of celebration.

What I did not give any thought to was the small things my girlfriend found so important, that I should have been more considerate about. Family pictures including my past wife on every wall and table surface in every room that was so delicately pointed out. These pictures were in outdated frames and quickly replaced with our recent adventures as a couple. I offered the old pictures to my children as they cherished the memories of their mother. Never used china in a curio cabinet with collectable family items from years past. We made room for her items of importance. To be fair, as any couple blends together, there needs to be compromise if the relationship continues to blossom. Don't sweat the small stuff, because the bigger decisions will be around the corner.

We were as a couple able to avoid difficult decisions other couples will need to decide as they blend households. Decisions that other couples making this commitment are: Moving from apartment to apartment with more space or who's house do we move into? Changing cities, neighborhoods, work may also play a role. Blending households and creating space for future grandchildren may also be a consideration? My Cousin (70 years old), decided to move with his girlfriend (72years old) in an upscale community twenty miles away. She was the cousin of his deceased wife. Both were retired and simply said, missed human connection. Yes, they missed hugs, kisses and conversation. The couple was handling it well, until the children stepped in posing opposition to the blending of household plan. The couple moved in together and lived happily ever after before she passed away. The extended family quickly asked my cousin, now 92 to move out of "their house". The extended family does not always play a role in the moving in process, but in by case we needed to set boundaries for my daughters. Moving forward, we told my daughters they needed to ring the door-bell or knock on the door before coming into the house. This did not sit well with my daughter, 26 who was used to coming and going as she pleased most of her life. The blending of household's process, donation of cherished items and buying new items together. Creating a yours, mine and ours is common. One event that stands out that demonstrated commitment and acceptance was a back deck "Man cave". We often shop at a local Farmers Saturday Market in our community where vendors sell food and their crafts. One Saturday morning, we attended the Saturday Market and leisurely walked by a wood furniture display including two benches, a chair, and side tables. The price was surprisingly affordable being hand made with the craftsman explaining it was his first Saturday market and he was testing the area. My girlfriend suggested it was a good deal and the furniture would fit perfect on the back deck where you could smoke cigars with your buddies. "A man cave…so to speak"! I thought about the idea for a moment, and she said "It's my gift to you, you will love it and so will your friends". I was not used to this generosity offered with such love and genuine caring. Fast forward to today, the deck furniture has had multiple cigar parties enjoying the furniture and I smoke in the "man cave" every night. We have since added some cigar posters and outdoor lights. Simply said, it has turned into a fun project we both now enjoy.

Moving forward; questions will be asked of one another during the transition, do we move into an existing place or find a new place of our own for a new start? The neighborhood needs to be considered too. Is the home going to be a house, condo, or an apartment? A rental is common at this stage of the relationship. How far is the home from family or to get away from stresses in life?

The decisions are endless and there is no right or wrong. In finding a new partner to move forward with in life we all sacrifice and make concessions. It's all a compromise.

The Proposal: ..... or get off the pot

It has been four years since we met, and the chemistry was right. We enjoy being with each other. Small gifts along the way with thought and sincerity are given. I mentioned the Saturday market in the prior section. At this community shopping event there is also a jeweler who displays his crafts. We walked by his booth several months earlier and my girlfriend fell in love with a ring with a Safire stone. The ring did not fit, but we were assured an easy fix. I came back without my girlfriend several hours later and bought the ring. I intended it to be an engagement ring, planning to propose within several months. I borrowed a ring my girlfriend rarely wore and used it as a sizing ring for the new engagement ring.

We also enjoy walking through pawn shops. Just interesting items no-one seems to really use or care about anymore. We found a ring my girlfriend liked, that again did not fit. There is a local jeweler in our community who does custom work. After several months of trying to design a ring for my girlfriend, we put that project on the side for a future. I asked the jeweler if she would look at the ring at the pawn shop and tell me if it is worth the price? If she agreed it was a good deal, we would buy it and have her custom size it. When my friend, the jeweler looked at the ring with a jeweler glass she indicated, it was well worth the price. We also learned it was called a kite ring, and needed to be rebuild to be sized correctly. Not what I wanted to hear; but looking back on this decision and the ring I see every day it was worth it.

After months of thought and planning, my girlfriend and I were on a drive back to Salem, Oregon from Portland, Oregon, about a forty-minute drive. She looked at me and said "are we ever going to get married?" I was not going to ruin my surprise and said "I don't really see a reason to." She said, then I need to make choices that's in my best interest." I understood at that moment, that day was the right day. I went to the flower shop and bought a dozen roses and card. I wrote in the card, "Will you marry me?" I'm not the formal guy, as you have learned through this process.

Her mother was at our house and they were preparing dinner. I came into the house from the back deck and as her mother was sitting at the kitchen table, gave my girlfriend the card and flowers. She had the look of utter surprise, what's this for? Did you do something wrong?

Her mother encouraged her to open the card, and as she did, she looked at me with Garfield eyes. She read out-loud, "Will You Marry me?" She looked at me with shock. "Well?" I said… She hugged me and said, "Yes!" I was so relieved. My now, fiancé looked at me and said, "and you planned this all along and had that conversation with me in the car this afternoon? How did you keep a straight face?"

Planning the wedding:

There are a few twists in this wedding planning, even I did not see coming. I wanted my fiancé to have the wedding of her dreams since she had never been married. But she wanted me to have the wedding of my dreams. As we planned a short engagement, we immediately let close family and friends know the good news. I told my daughters and brother the news of our engagement. My brother and youngest daughter were both excited for us. My oldest daughter, asked why? She gave Jen a hug and said congratulations? She was not supportive of my dating so soon after her mother passed. I won't go into details at this level, but as I said earlier in the book, family support is not always going to be what we expect.

Jen and I talked about a simple wedding, calling a Justice of the Peace and having a short non-formal wedding on the Courthouse steps. Simple outfit for both with a simple flower arrangement and a witness. Being that we were in the middle of a pandemic we knew our options were limited at best. Thankfully, this aligned with Jen's desires for something very simple.

Then Jen offered an idea, 'why don't we have a Jewish wedding'? Perhaps at your Synagogue in Salem? I was raised in a Reform Jewish house. I attended a Reform Temple in Los Angeles, Wilshire BL. Temple. A highly liberal temple with relaxed rituals at the time. Friday evening Shabot services were usually a tolerable forty-five minutes long. My first wedding at age thirty, was in a restaurant and officiated by a Cantor. "Let me do my homework on this idea," I replied. Very comforting thought to think of an actual Jewish ceremony.

I reached out to the Reconstruction Synagogue in Salem. Reconstruction is a blend of old and new, leaning toward conservative faith based Jewish teachings. Services in a Reconstruction or Conservative Jewish Synagogue can last one to three hours. As a child, a five- minute service was too long. I called and asked if the Rabbi at the Salem Temple would officiate our wedding? I was a past member and they remembered me. I was asked if I was marrying a Jewish girl? No, I said and the person replied that the Rabbi is busy with High Holy holiday planning during October. The search continues.

I reached out to a friend and colleague in Portland, Oregon who practiced the Reform tradition as I did and he recommended a Reform Temple in Portland. I visited the Temple and was given the same response. Jen had a great thought regarding a Jewish wedding, but I was hitting a brick wall. Then it occurred to me, many years ago when I arrived in Oregon, I attended a Reform Temple in Corvallis, Oregon. I reached out to Temple Am Bet and they asked similar questions. Is your fiancé' Jewish? No, I said. Their reply, no worries. Are you a member? No, but I am willing to make a generous donation. We would love that they said; the Rabbi will call you back when he returns. Two days later we had an hour conversation on the phone followed by a Zoom call and the Rabbi agreed to perform our wedding. A few rituals were completed including buying a Ketubah (Wedding Vows in a Jewish certification) with no problem and the wedding date was set.

Oh my, this is really happening? My emotions were running on high realizing I was going to get married for the second time. The following couple of days, Jen was unhappy crying on and off with no explanation and I let it go. Finally, I asked what was wrong and what could I do to help? She informed me that her cousins are JW (Jehovah Witness) and it is against their belief to attend weddings. Jen said, "I'm sure They won't attend our wedding." I asked, "can we invite them?" She replied, we can, but they will just say No. . I asked Jen for approval to call and have a conversation with her family? I suggested, they definitely won't come, if not invited. She agreed. I called her cousin and asked for a conversation; he asked if this conversation was with Jen's blessing? Yes, I said. I am inviting you to our wedding. Jen said your JW and don't attend weddings. He agreed, this is true. So, I said, Jen has been crying for two days as a result of this ritual you have. I don't understand it , but I do respect it. I did my part by inviting you, it's up to you if you attend or not. Her cousin asked if he could think about it for 24 hours? I said, take all the time you want. The next day her cousin called me back; I was thrilled, "we would be honored to attend your wedding". Great I said, the invitation will be on the way soon. I told Jen, her family will attend her wedding. She was beyond thrilled! So nice when we can work as a team.

Planning the Wedding

We needed a male non-relative Jewish witness and discovered in conversation the man who sold us coffee at the Saturday Market was Jewish. He agreed to be our witness after a lengthy conversation. The Temple had the Chuppah (Canopy to take our Wedding Vows Under) and the covered outside area of the Temple was reserved due to the pandemic.

Our wedding day arrived and the Zoom camera and Chuppah was set up. Jen came out of the Temple with her mother dressed in a blue dress with a white and blue shoulder covering. Absolutely beautiful. My children arrived and my oldest daughter was clearly having trouble wrapping her head around this moment. We turned on the Zoom camera link to see the faces of relatives and family from around the country. Covid was at a high population count and without modern technology this day would not have had the same emotional connection. The marriage license was signed and the Chuppah was erected. The service was delightful in every sense of the word. I was the luckiest man in the world at that moment. At the conclusion of the ceremony, I broke the wine glass and yelled "Mussel-Tov". Just the thought a woman I met a few years ago would embrace my faith and up-bringing and allow us to have a Jewish Wedding meant the world to me. Her mother, now my mother-in-law is a practicing Christian and accepted me with open arms into the family. I wish I could say, all family's embrace different cultures in the same light, but I know better. My best man at my first wedding is of the Catholic faith, and it does not have any impact on our friendship. I too was the best man at his wedding, and he needed to get a Catholic witness.. We all need to respect differences as we meet and cultivate new relationships.

As time wanders on, we recognized that we needed to create new Wills. What was mine is now ours and what is Jen's is now ours. My children are clearly still part of my life, but when I die there will be a division of my retirement with my new family. I highly recommend a Trust or Will be set up after a wedding or after years of time together as new laws are passed regarding communion. Families are destroyed as a result of no planning or communication.

As a gift to ourselves we bought a vacation house in our favorite town on the coast. I sold an investment property and used the earnings to purchase our vacation home and property we both fell in love with. The house needed an extensive renovation and as a newlywed couple we brought our resources together and shared in repair costs. I am a minimalist and did not want to clutter the home at first with furniture and nick-knacks. We agreed to furnish the home with yours, mine, and our furniture. We brought in my parent's old moss green couch with sentimental value and covered it with a ten -dollar couch cover to match the white paint. Jen offered a red love seat and large chair from a living-room set she brought from her home. We bought two chairs from Costco to complete the living room. We enjoy garage sales and bargain hunting and found a small four seat kitchen table set and simple six chair dinette set to establish a dining area. My mother-in-law contributed two new king beds and my parent's old bed was set up in the guest room. Pictures we had left over from Jen's move and pictures I took from local attractions hang on the walls. It is a gift to last into our retirement down the road.

Conclusion

I introduced you to how I met my first wife in my twenties and the evolution of our relationship till the end. I intended to open your eyes into how we think in our youth searching for a better half, sometimes unintentionally. We can't predict the future, nor should we because that would be trying to predict life. I then evolved into my un-intended search to replace the hugs, kisses, and conversation I was so desperately missing, after my wife passed away. I gave examples of how people find themselves alone as a widower, widow, or divorced and a brief understanding of how chemistry plays a role in finding once again that human connection. I introduced later on in my book my experiences of how holding hands was unintentionally left out, and as important if not more important than the hugs, kisses, and conversation. We walked through looking around our environment and people watching. We established our next relationship could be standing next to us.

I intentionally, did not go into depth about the chemistry of the brain and what happens when we first see a partner, embrace the first hug, the first kiss, have that initial conversation, and eventually hold each other's hands. It appeared to me delving deep into the chemistry was just filling pages and that is not my intention. I believe we can use Google for that search and dive into endless studies and books for those answers. In the long term of the new relationship, I believe I established that chemistry happens naturally, it is not for us to question.

I suggested using Dating services, meeting in common areas of interest (hiking, school classes, and involving friends (blind dates) as perhaps an avenue to find a partner. The path to intimacy is so personal and common sense must be practiced in this evolution of the new relationship.

How to grow in a relationship was shared using myself as an example and eventually the commitment from both parties involved. I covered the moving in together and how I shared my answer to joining households.

I decided to get married, yet at this stage in life that is not always the best option. Retirement benefits and local laws should be seriously looked into to decide if this benefits your extended family.

I am so thrilled to have shared my journey and finding my new partner in life. It is so individual and the journey to find a new partner starts the second you walk out of your door. You get the idea.

As I close my book, I want to share an experience that happened this past weekend. This story ties everything together and makes several key points.

I was with my wife driving very slow on a community road in total darkness with my car lights on returning home from swimming. I was distracted for a moment making a wide left turn and hit something hearing my engine revving from being knocked out of gear and the thump of a flat tire. No structures or animals were seen. I limped my car back home fifty yards away. I returned back in the darkness to see a cement barrier in a gully, I must have accidently hit making a wide turn.

My wife kept her composure saying, accidents happen. We have AAA for free towing from the coast back to the valley. You bought your tires from Less Schwab, local tire center and should be covered.

We understood other Wholesale stores were less expensive, but with limited locations. I was beating myself up for the issue I created and was constantly reminded, we can take care of the tire tomorrow, Sunday morning. Jen was hoping we didn't cause transmission or wheel damage? The next morning, we used AAA and had a successful tow back to the valley. The operator put on our spare tire when we returned home. The spare tire is referred to for a ten-mile radius and no faster than fifty miles an hour. It would not have lasted the seventy-mile return home. I took my tire into our local tire center for a free replacement.

I post this because it speaks so much about a chemistry, co-operation, and caring. Immediately following the incident, we did not argue playing a blame game. I had Jennifer's full support and confidence. We agreed early on that buying car tires at a locally owned and supported tire center was a little more money, but gave us full support and service. I recommend the AAA service that has never failed me. Local insurance companies have similar coverage, but AAA worked for me over 50 years. This is a simple example of what a working relationship looks like.

Have fun with ice breaker questions as you explore each other's personality

- What was (is) your nick name growing up?
- What do you like collecting?
- How did you and your best friend meet?
- What is your Astrological sign? Do you think it Is it accurate in its description of you?
- What makes you happy and smile?
- What is your favorite color?
- What is your top three favorite songs?
- What are your hobbies?
- What is your occupation and is it work or pleasure?
- What pets do you have and what are their names?
- Do you have children? What traits did they get from you?
- What is your faith and are you active in rituals?
- What is your eye color and favorite perfume and cologne?
- Continue asking fun questions as you explore each other's personalities.

Excerpt: From eldest daughter

───◆───

Hi, my name is Sharon. My Dad asked me to add my perspective on what life was like living with my Mom, an individual who had a mental illness she was diagnosed with at 21.

I remember her telling me stories of her childhood, especially being excited to move out with a boyfriend Larry and her mom cried in the open garage as she left. She knew something was different about her and checked herself into a mental health place to be diagnosed. We believe her mom is undiagnosed Maniac Depressive, however my Grandma firmly believes she just likes to talk and that there's nothing wrong with that. I chuckle at that because her "likes to talk" is usually most of an hour with the other person adding very little.

I didn't find anything odd about my childhood. My parents were a team; my dad worked during the week to support us while my mom was home and free to do as she pleased. We would all go out during the weekend to Silver Falls for hikes or Soccer games for either my younger sister Megan or I. They would take turns making dinner and washing the dishes. The only difference between our family and the couple friend's families I was close to was my dad seemed to be more in charge and my friend's moms seemed to run things for their family, whether they were the "bread winner" or not.

I had a strange year when I was about 8. I had a year of Déjà vu. Certain events seem to happen consistently like the year before. When I turned 9, I wondered if it would happen again, but life changed drastically. We'd had a dog we named Buddy who one day was drinking slowly nonstop for about 5 minutes. I thought it was strange. My mom said he looked like an Ethiopian baby. I'm still not sure what she meant, but his stomach had begun to swell on the sides. We ended up putting him down.

My mom started to gain weight oddly. I remember her explaining it as "I had a salad and gained 10 pounds!" Mind you, she was a bit of an over-exaggerator like her mom, so I'm not sure how accurate *that* statement is. The point is, she gained unexplained weight consistently that year. My dad took her to 3 doctors that I remember hearing about: one said to push away from the table (I heard my dad almost decked him, and he isn't violent), one said he didn't know what was wrong, and the final one was an Endocrinologist who would end up being her doctor for the next 14 years. He said he knew what she had, that it was very rare in humans and it usually happens in dogs. We learned about Cushing's Disease that year.

Before my dad took my mom to doctors to find out what was wrong, they sat me down and told me she had Bi-Polar or was a Maniac Depressive. They explained these two phrases meant the same thing, essentially it affected her moods, but she was on medication and I didn't have to worry about anything. But whatever was now going on might affect that and they thought I was old enough to know what was going on so I could watch over my then 6-year-old sister without question when he took her to an appointment to try to find an answer.

I was 10 when we finally knew what was going on so we could figure out a plan of action. Unfortunately, it wasn't simple. There is no cure for Cushings disease, only medical band aids. We learned she had a pituitary tumor and did surgery to remove it. As a result, the doctor added a medication to her already growing medication list to stabilize her moods. When the Cushing's disease returned, they doctors decided one more option was left to removed her Adrenal glands.

I remember my mom sleeping a lot. I called her a Seasonal Maniac Depressive—Maniac when it was hot and Depressive when it was cold. Summer was June-Aug and then it would get very cold. I remember her not getting up really for about a month (must have been Fall) and she woke up in the mornings for one week. I must have been about 11 or 12 years old and my sister was 8 or 9 years old. Megan went into their bedroom to check on our mom and was asked to do something. I heard my mom ask and my sister's response, "I need to ask Sharon." She then ran to me to deliver the message of what mom wanted and ask my permission (since she was my helper when dad was at work and mom wasn't up). I told her "Yes, but while Mom's up, you don't need to ask my permission. Just do as she asks." "Ok!" she responded.

This happened consistently all week. The second day, my mom was worried and told her, "Sharon's not your boss." Megan still ran out of the room to me and repeated the request and asked for permission, adding what mom said at the end, confused. By the end of the week, and being told the same thing over and over, it started settling in her mind. The morning that I knew was coming arrived. Mom didn't wake up. I asked Megan for help with laundry as usual and she said in a more realized voice, "Mom said you're not my boss." It was time to get real with her. "Look, Mom's not waking up today. I need your help." Thankfully, she did her "Ok!" and we continued the day like normal.

One of the hardest things was having friends over. A friend I met in Grade school and my best friend from Middle school were really the only two people I let come over around my mom. They had patience and understanding with her, especially when she wasn't quite there mentally.

At the end of the day, even through the last 3-5 years of her life when she started to be mentally gone more than here, she was my support. She was my guide. We'd go over Pros and Cons and whatever

I decided, she would help me down that path. My dad and sister do not have long patience fuses. Out of frustration, they yelled at her constantly. I was the mediator; I would defend my mom against them. And (regardless of her state of mind) when they would verbally attack me, she would defend me. The only difference was ammo she used. She wasn't too mean when she was in her right state of mind, but she got cruel if she was gone.

Her last best friend said she'd always be there for her. In the summer of 2012, I went to Yellowstone, WY for a few months and received a picture from her over text of a bruise on my sister's arm. I asked what my sister did. I knew it wasn't my mom's fault, that she'd been provoked. I was told my mom had gone for her wallet and Megan had taken it. With the velocity of movement, my mom's hand smacked her just the right way and bruised her. It didn't surprise me. I knew Megan was trying to keep her from getting in trouble with our dad, but I told her and Megan to just give her back her wallet. My Dad would deal with it later.

A little after I came back home, she reached out to my mom and us claiming she was so sorry, but she had to pull away from our family. She first said she had joined a volunteer program with the fire department and they had a rule (much like police) that if they witnessed violence, they were instructed to report it. She said she knew it wasn't my mom's fault and didn't want to get her into trouble. She also said she had to protect her own family, which didn't seem congruent. She later told me that the event with my sister had scared one of her daughters and that was part of the reason to "protect her family".

The last week of my mom's life in the hospital, I went to visit her every day from 11am-3pm. The first 3 days, she was very alert. A friend of Megan's and I who had helped with her, came by to say hi a couple times and stayed an hour or two each time. My best friend dropped by once on a break from work to say hi to my mom and to check on me. I texted my mom's friend the second day that she was in the regular hospital and not doing well. I don't remember getting a response that time. The fourth day, she was fading and I texted her friend in the evening that she should really visit my mom if she really cared about her (essentially my mom was not doing well). She simply replied she was feeding her family dinner. I told her she may not have more than 3 more days left, unless her body pulled through.

She showed up the 5th day, my mom's last night with us. She had been sleeping most of the day. My dad met her at the door and asked what the hell she was doing there. I heard her say she came to say goodbye and be there for us girls. I was honestly surprised she showed up. She tried helping us take off my mom's 2 rings on her ring fingers, but we only got one off. Aside from other drama that doesn't pertain to this, my family is still not very close with her after her decision to abandon my mom.

It's been 7 years since my mom passed, Aug 26, 2015. The first year left a huge void in my life, no more music blasting in the house, no more random movies to keep her entertained, no more shows to enjoy with her. She and I were movie buffs, I didn't realize how much we watched until I attempted to watch shows without her for the first time. I'm still finding movies and shows I haven't watched since she was on the couch next to me.

My husband listens to my stories about my mom and has seen her pictures. He may not have met her, but he understands my connection with her better than most guys in his position. He is my light now and he gave me back that support that I lost 7 years ago, and I'm utterly grateful to him for it.

Epilogue

First and foremost, thank you for investing your time into reading or at least glancing at my book. I have read several books in my life and yes, guilty as charged, glanced at the introduction or the last page of a book only to determine it was not of interest to look beyond. So, if you're like me, go ahead and explore my work for the rough edges, glance at the last page, explore the back of the book for the reason I wrote this and decide if you want to spend some time with me. I'm honored you even picked up my book and or asked me for a sneak peek. I have a story to tell that is highly personal, yet I feel important to share in today's dating circle of forty, fifty, and sixty-year old's plus in age. Circumstances beyond our control leaving us as widowers, widows, and divorcees.

I write these pages to share with you my journey. In doing so I have recognized my own personal prejudices and bias, which you may recognize and relate to or take offence. I share these things not to offend anyone, but to give an honest window into life with a loved one living with mental illness. This perspective is not one from a clinical side; I did not study or practice mental health treatment, and this is not intended to offend those who do treat people with mental illness. This is coming from a person that had to watch a cherished loved one suffer from the effects of mental and physical illness, as well as the effects on those around them.

Ice Breaker Questions

Have fun with ice breaker questions as you explore each other's personality

- What was (is) your nick name growing up?

- What do you like collecting?

- How did you and your best friend meet?

- What is your Astrological sign? Do you think it Is it accurate in its description of you?

- What makes you happy and smile?

- What is your favorite color?

- What is your top three favorite songs?

- What are your hobbies?

- What is your occupation and is it work or pleasure?

- What pets do you have and what are their names?

- Do you have children? What traits did they get from you?

- What is your faith and are you active in rituals?

- What is your eye color and favorite perfume and cologne?

- Continue asking fun questions as you explore each other's personalities.

About the Author

Allen lived in Los Angeles county for thirty-eight years were he started his career in healthcare as an Emergency Room EMT. Shortly after starting college, he met his wife Linda and they had two daughters. They relocated to the Northwest for an outdoor lifestyle.

Today, he is happily married to his second wife Jennifer, waiting for the arrival of twin grandchildren from his oldest, and watching the success of his youngest. He enjoys fine cigars and the friendships within the cigar lounge community. The pictures on the front and back of the book are their happy place.

Please enjoy I MISS: Hugs, Kisses, and Conversation with an open mind and full heart. I encourage you to share your thoughts and I am open to consulting projects.

I studied Speech Communication/Rhetoric at California State University Northridge graduating with a BA.

I am an active member of Toastmasters International participating in leadership and speech contests.

My career in life science sales and brand marketing, has been enriched through my skills promoting to the healthcare industry.

I would be honored to present at any public event or life science conference in person or Virtual.

Living with mental health in the family.

Dating forty and beyond.

Why would anyone want to listen to what I have to say? Sales

Reach out to me through LinkedIn or email for a conversation.

Joiningscienceandmedicine@gmail.com

https://www.linkedin.com/in/allen-prell-cmr-34966822

PO Box 7608

Salem, OR 97303

Made in the USA
Columbia, SC
24 May 2023